Supporting Workplace Learning with Neuroscience

Developing Expertise in Organizations

Seth-Aaron Martinez

Routledge
Taylor & Francis Group
NEW YORK AND LONDON

Designed cover image: Getty Images

First published 2026
by Routledge
605 Third Avenue, New York, NY 10158

and by Routledge
4 Park Square, Milton Park, Abingdon, Oxon OX14 4RN

Routledge is an imprint of the Taylor & Francis Group, an informa business

Library of Congress Cataloging-in-Publication Data
A catalog record for this title has been requested

ISBN: 9781032974163 (hbk)
ISBN: 9781032974156 (pbk)
ISBN: 9781003593607 (ebk)

DOI: 10.4324/9781003593607

Typeset in Galliard
by Taylor & Francis Books

Contents

Illustrations

Figures

Tables

Preface

Adult learning plays a crucial role in helping organizations adapt to change by supporting employees in their development of the knowledge, skills, and abilities related to their craft. The primary aim of this book is to provide you with information that explains and enhances such learning in professional settings. In this manner, this book is part science and part theory. However, at the end of each chapter I will share a layer of tactics regarding how to potentially apply these principles of learning in practice. These application sections will be based in part by scholarship, in part by my research, and in part by my experiences in industry. Taken together, this book is fundamentally based on two sources of information: (1) peer-reviewed research and theoretical scholarship from the fields of neuroscience, cognitive psychology, and adult learning science (including my own research); and (2) my professional experience in the field.

What This Book Is and Is Not

Please consider this book a resource for anyone interested in adult learning and developing expertise, especially those who plan a career in professional learning and development (L&D). This book is meant to provide you with a foundation of adult learning science principles and concepts. But to be clear, in writing this book I deviate from traditional treatments of adult learning. Most textbooks begin by covering an abundance of theories; however, I do not. Instead, I organize the book around three key dimensions of learning (i.e. cognitive, behavioral, socio-emotional), which are introduced in greater detail in Chapter One. Next, because this book is rooted in science and research, there is less room for error. I say this because many heavily used books on these topics contain sections that are now known to be somewhat inaccurate in some cases, or downright false in others. It is my hope and belief that the book that I have written is free of such inaccuracies or falsities.

Learning and Development Is an Applied Field

The field of L&D is an applied field. As such, I am not overly concerned with providing you a heavy dose of theoretical concepts with minimal connection to practical work and true impact. Instead, I would much rather you read this book with the mindset, "How can I take what is known and apply it to my work?" So while I introduce several theories in this book, my focus is less on theory, per se, and much more on what is definitively known scientifically (i.e. through rigorous research) about adult learning and what that knowledge means for practice.

A Note about Theory

Additionally, I want to take a moment to further consider the role of theory and its relevance to practitioners in the fields of L&D and workplace performance improvement. The value of theory is to make the human experience intelligible (Eaton, 1921). In other words, a strong theory is one that provides a sound explanation, model, or schema of a phenomenon that you and I experience. Additionally, Iowa State University professor Dr. John Wacker (1998) considered the fundamental purpose of theory to be to build a body of knowledge that can be applied across a variety of situations. In Dr. Wacker's view, a good theory explains the what, when, where, and why certain phenomena will occur. He goes on to explain that three elements define what a good theory needs to include to accomplish this objective:

- A quality theory provides a framework for analysis and discussion in a field.
- A quality theory informs the rationale behind practical and operational practices.
- A quality theory serves as the foundation for future research and field development.

Worded simply, the value of a quality theory rests entirely in its *explanatory* power. The more a theory can explain a phenomenon, the better the theory; the more varied and different the situations in which a theory can explain the phenomenon, the better the theory (Van de Ven, 1989; Whetten, 1989).

I share all of this to position the role of theory in the development this book. To be clear, the principal goal of both my research lab work since becoming a professor and my approach to writing this book which began in summer 2023 was to extract and communicate everything known about adult learning based on research and science. However, in composing this book it was clear that there are moments when theory absolutely has a place and, therefore, must be recognized and discussed. So, while most of this book is founded on rigorous, scientific research, you will find that I still include a number of theories that are highly relevant today.

My Position as Author

Each of us possesses a unique identity and bring with us an equally unique personal background and work history. As stated above, the writing approach and tone of this book is based largely on my professional experiences and how I view workplace learning as a result. Therefore, before advancing further I should introduce myself and share my background. The hope is that in doing so as the reader you know the point of view I bring, so that you have maximum context for the book's contents. Thus, for the sake of credibility I briefly offer my professional experience.

First, I love the study of learning—it is a fascination that began as a service missionary in my early twenties and continued through my undergraduate degree. As I approached graduation and began considering graduate school, I knew I wanted to further study something related to the human body. But what I did not anticipate was how much of a lightbulb went off for me when I focused on the human brain and learning—it was a genuine fascination with the topic. And that lightbulb has been shining bright ever since.

After I obtained my MS in instructional psychology from Brigham Young University, I pursued a PhD in instructional systems from Indiana University. In both my master's and doctorate, I was exposed to principles of adult learning. Following the completion of my doctorate, I accepted a role at the Graduate School of Business at Stanford University, where I consulted internally with faculty to design MBA and executive education courses.

After Stanford, I spent three years at Adobe managing a machine learning training program for all Adobe software engineers and data scientists globally. My most recent industry position was at Meta where my team of senior learning strategists supported the learning and performance of the 40,000 content moderators that Meta employed to keep harmful content off Facebook and Instagram pages.

As I look back, the consistent thread interwoven through my 10 years of professional experience before transitioning back to academia has always been my love of adult learning and the exploration of how individuals can optimally learn and develop. Not only did this love pull me back to academia, but it drives the courses I teach and further impacts the projects I choose to work on in my research lab.

The Organizational Strategy of this Book

This book begins with three chapters that provide context for the remaining chapters. Chapter 1 provides an overview about the relationship between *adult learning* and *performance*. Chapter 2 then unpacks the nature of *expertise* and how it is optimally *developed*. Chapter 3 introduces *neurodiversity*, *culture*, and *ethics*—three considerations that are deeply relevant to our work as professionals. In sum, the first three context-providing chapters provide a guiding framework from which to proceed with the remainder of the book.

Then, as stated above, the core of this book is organized according to three fundamental dimensions of adult learning: cognitive, behavioral, and socio-emotional. The cognitive dimension is comprised of four distinct chapters. Chapter 4 offers the anatomical features of our *central nervous system* and how those parts contribute to *memory*. Chapter 5 next focuses on adult *neuroplasticity*, which is the brain's ability to adapt, learn, and grow based on experiencing the world. Chapter 6 centers on *metacognition*, which is a person's awareness and understanding of their own thought processes. The focus of Chapter 7 is learning through audio-visual means from *technology* and *multimedia*.

Following the four cognitive dimension chapters, the book then shifts to two chapters on the behavioral dimension of adult learning. Chapter 8 centers on the theory of *behaviorism* and covers all things related to *behavioral* (or *skill-based*) performances. Chapter 9 then focuses exclusively on *motivation*.

The socioemotional dimension is the third dimension of adult learning and consists of two chapters. Chapter 10 covers the theories of *social constructivism* and *social learning*, while Chapter 11 covers the role of *emotion* in the learning process.

The final two chapters of the book are broad in nature. Chapter 12 deals with several topics to further assist a professional who aspires to design optimal learning experiences. It dispels several myths that have prevailed in the L&D world, introduces Merrill's classic *First Principles of Instruction*, as well as covering *storytelling* and the *universal design for learning* (UDL). Chapter 13 discusses several near-future trends in adult learning in the workplace.

References

Eaton, R. M. (1921). The value of theories. *The Journal of Philosophy*, 18(25), 682–690.

Van de Ven, A. H. (1989). Nothing is quite so practical as a good theory. *Academy of Management Review*, 14(4), 486–489.

Wacker, J. G. (1998). A definition of theory: research guidelines for different theory building research methods in operations management. *Journal of Operations Management*, 16(4), 361–385. doi:10.1016/s0272-6963(98)00019-00019.

Whetten, D. A. (1989). What constitutes a theoretical contribution? *Academy of Management Review*, 14(4), 490–495.

Acknowledgements

I would like to acknowledge and thank the members of my Learning Strategy Lab who assisted greatly in the principal work leading to this book. Those special contributors include: Sumaya Ali, LaKell Archer, John Arenas, Melanie Bray-Beardall, John Buwalda, Jessie Clark, Matt Engle, Maryam Hussain, Emma Indart, Karyna Mangusheva, Halah Mohammed, Gaby Nazario Ramos, and Danielle Wachter.

Part I

Establishing the Context

1 What Is Adult Learning and Performance?

Within the workplace setting, the phenomenon of training and developing employees is often referred to as *performance improvement*. However, at one of my previous employers, my team's name was *Global Talent Development*. At another employer, we were *Digital Learning Solutions*. In my most recent role at Meta, my team of senior learning strategists was part of the *Global Learning Organization*. Currently, the professional organization for which I most often attend and publish is known as the *Academy of Human Resource Development*. Given such different names, it would be natural to wonder if my duties and remit were significantly different from role to role, organization to organization. Well, yes, these roles were different; however, the knowledge, skills, and abilities required to succeed in each role did not vary a great deal. The natural question arises, "Why are there so many different names and labels used when the actual job duties themselves are more similar than dissimilar?"

As I look back over my professional life, initially working as an early-career instructional designer across several different universities, then at the headquarters of a global religious organization, then later as a learning experience designer at the Stanford Graduate School of Business, a global training program manager at Adobe, and most recently as a senior learning strategist at Meta, I have found that the skills required to succeed from one role to the next are highly transferable. That is, I was able to advance in these different roles by leveraging many of the skills required from the previous roles—the overlap was strong. Moreover, I consistently observed a specific attribute that the best performers possessed at each organization: in key meetings and discussions where important strategic decisions needed to be made, the top performers would always be those individuals who stated, "For this situation, research suggests that it is best to [insert a principle of learning]," or "Adult cognition is enhanced when [insert neuroscientific fact], so therefore we should do X, but not do Z." In my experience, statements such as these were essentially mic-drop statements, against which no one in the meeting would challenge or refute, including directors or VPs. I observed this pattern with such consistency that I began to adopt the practice myself initially, and now fully swear by it. Therefore, to be clear, the purpose of this book is to help you become one of those top performers yourself by understanding the key principles of adult learning and applying them as professionals to help others develop into top performers themselves as well.

This chapter opens by establishing the workplace context in which we find ourselves. We discuss an organization's primary interest in developing the talent of their employees–namely, their employees' individual and collective expertise–with the ultimate goal of improving their job performance. We explore the various terms and synonyms that one might encounter in the field, paying particular attention to the relationship to adult learning for each. We will consider labels such as expertise development, talent development, learning and development, the transfer of training, and several others. Lastly, this and every remaining chapter concludes with a section devoted to the key take-aways and applications of the chapter's main concepts for a practitioner.

DOI: 10.4324/9781003593607-2

Before Discussing Learning, We Must First Understand Performance

A chief concern for any organization is the optimal performance of its employees or members. Optimal performance includes efficient execution (i.e. getting things done at a high rate) combined with optimal quality (i.e. getting those things done well). The logic is simple: if individuals and teams perform at a top level, then the organization, in turn, will likely perform at a top level as well. In other words, the high performance of the parts leads to the high performance of the whole—high performance begets high performance. Research shows that organizations who invest in employee learning and development see greater employee satisfaction and retention (Lee & Bruvold, 2003), and a more skilled and adaptable workforce from which to hire (Hameed & Waheed, 2011). So ultimately, the effective application of learning principles serves to benefit both the individual and the organization (Dachner et al., 2021). It becomes a win–win.

Yet despite this common goal of top performance, different organizations refer to this phenomenon in different ways using different terminology, as I described above. Therefore, to best establish a clear foundation it is important that I begin by attending to these similar, yet different, terms and labels.

Performance Improvement and Human Performance Technology

Performance improvement (PI) consists of exactly what it implies—improving the performance of individuals, teams, and organizations, including the processes involved at each level (Rummler & Brache, 1992). As a field, PI relies on evidence and data to inform decisions that are both systemic (i.e. considers the entire organization) and systematic (i.e. methodical, thorough). PI is interdisciplinary, borrowing from the disciplines of psychology, management, economics, and systems theory (Swanson, 1999).

Closely related to PI is the field of human performance technology (HPT), a systematic approach used to improve performance within organizations by analyzing the human and organizational factors that contribute to effectiveness. HPT identifies gaps between desired and current performance, analyzes root causes, and implements solutions that enhance individual and group performance levels. Like PI, HPT draws on principles from multiple disciplines, including psychology, education, and business management.

HPT assists organizations by conducting performance analyses and tests, supporting employee selection, training, and motivation, and reorganizing work environments to facilitate better performance (Eren, 2014). The model outlined by Eren highlights key phases within HPT, particularly the performance analysis and cause analysis stages, which help identify factors such as inadequate equipment or low morale that might prevent optimal performance (Eren, 2014). This illustrates that HPT operates not just on enhancing processes but also on directly addressing human needs and organizational culture to foster engagement.

Effective performance measurement is also integral to both PI and HPT. Klovienė and Uosytė (2019) argued that organizations must develop performance measurement systems that are responsive to rapid changes and innovative trends. This adaptability is crucial for organizations navigating the complexities of modern business environments, particularly in the context of Industry 4.0, where technology and rapid changes demand agile strategies for improvement (Yadav et al., 2020).

In essence, PI and HPT create a structured and data-driven process for enhancing performance across organizations with a focus on the interplay of human, technological, and organizational factors. By systematically analyzing performance gaps and implementing tailored interventions, PI and HPT enable organizations to achieve higher efficacy and efficiency, ultimately enhancing overall productivity. The leading professional organization focused on PI and HPT is the International Society for Performance Improvement (ISPI).

Expertise Development

Our understanding of expertise development stems from the field of psychology. The field of expertise development focuses on improving the knowledge and skills of individuals within an organization to enhance their performance. (Do you start to see a pattern?) Expertise development encompasses various components, including training strategies, job design, and organizational learning, all aimed at fostering employee capabilities that are aligned with strategic goals. A significant review of scholarly literature by Farrington-Darby and Wilson (2006) synthesized decades of research on expertise into a concise definition. According to these scholars, expertise refers to the skills, knowledge, or abilities that are required for tasks, activities, jobs, and sport. Expertise can refer to a process (e.g. decision making) or it can refer to an output (e. g. a decision). It is worth noting here that according to their definition expertise refers to one's *knowledge, skills*, and *abilities*—a trio which is commonly referred to as "KSAs" in the management and organizational behavior literature. (For simplicity, from here onward I will refer to the trio of knowledge, skills, and abilities as KSAs.) It is also important to highlight that expertise manifests itself as both (1) a process, or (2) the outcome of said process.

Talent Development

Interestingly, in the scholarly literature the specific phrase "talent development" is often used in relation to the abilities or giftedness of children and adolescents. In the working world, however, the term talent development does not pertain to children or adolescents. Instead, it is used in place of the notion of expertise development for employees. Do you recall that *Global Talent Development* was the title of my learning team at Adobe? Yet for all intents and purposes, my team was entirely focused on developing the expertise of the employees at Adobe across a variety of topics. The key organization focusing on talent development in North America is the Association for Talent Development (ATD).

Human Resource Development

Very closely related to the development of expertise and talent is Human Resource Development (HRD). As a discipline, HRD falls within the broader scope of management and organizational studies, encompassing various practices and processes aimed at enhancing individual and organizational effectiveness. HRD is particularly concerned with the development of employee capabilities (i.e. KSAs) through training, education, and career development initiatives that align with the strategic goals of the organization. To that end, HRD leverages learning-related activities to shape individual and team values, beliefs, and skill development which support the desired performance of the larger organization (Wang et al., 2017). This definition essentially means that HRD is concerned with shaping the KSA's of individuals and teams to ultimately benefit the performance of the organization. The chief professional organization interested in HRD in the United States is the Academy of Human Resource Development (AHRD).

Combining Them All

Are you beginning to see a pattern? The terms described above—performance improvement, expertise development, talent development, human resource development—each relate to slightly different fields with slightly different origins. However, when all is said and done (and this is the key point to take away), each is fundamentally concerned with the exact same phenomenon: the learning, growth, and development of the people that

compose an organization. On this idea, Dachner et al. (2021) stated that employee development is the increased capacity of an individual to perform his or her current or future job. Formal development activities include classroom instruction, on-line courses, college degree programs, and mentorship programs, systematically designed with specific goals, learning objectives, assessment instruments, and expectations (Chen & Klimoski, 2007). Ultimately, should you encounter these terms used interchangeably in the professional world there is no need to worry or be confused, because each of these terms and fields converge at the core that is *adult learning*.

What Does "Learning" Mean?

In a basic sense, learning is the process of forming an internal model of the external world (i.e. our environment). Mental models of the external world, therefore, form the foundation of our conceptualization of learning. But to be more robust, Dehaene (2021) set forth several specific attributes of learning that provide a more nuanced view:

1. Learning is adjusting the parameters of a mental model;
2. Learning is minimizing errors while optimizing a reward function;
3. Learning is exploring the space of possibilities;
4. Learning is inferring the grammar of a domain.

I will consider each of these four definitions of the phenomenon known as "learning."

1 Learning is Adjusting the Parameters of a Mental Model

Definition of Mental Models

The processes of adult reasoning—which includes learning, understanding, problem solving, etc.—are a product of the individual's mental models (Fischbein et al., 1990). A *mental model* is an internal, cognitive structure that represents an external reality (Jones et al., 2011). A mental model can represent an event, an object, a subject area, or anything that the mind is thinking about (Ericsson & Pool, 2016; Jacob & Shaw, 1998). Mental models allow individuals to understand, explain, predict, and draw inferences from the behavior and events in the world around them (Mathieu et al., 2000). Mental models are conceptual representations in the mind and are therefore often referred to as "mental representations," "mental constructs," or "schemas." Our brains use mental models to sidestep the usual restrictions that memory places on mental processing (Sweller, 1994). (I will discuss memory in greater detail in Chapter 4.) Specifically, mental models reflect pre-existing patterns of information that are held in our long-term memory which can be used to respond quickly and effectively in certain types of situations. Consider this basic description of mental models or schemas by Sweller, who uses the basic idea of a tree:

> For example, consider schemas that deal with common objects such as trees. No two trees have identical elements but each tree can be instantly incorporated into a tree schema. As a consequence, if asked to describe a particular tree from memory, a person's description will be heavily influenced by a tree schema rather than entirely by the particular tree elements (leaves, branches, colour, etc.) actually seen. Tree schemas allow people to deal effortlessly with the potentially infinite variety of objects called trees. In a similar manner, there are schemas for dealing with problems. These schemas

> allow the classification of problems into categories according to how they will be dealt with.
>
> (Sweller, 1994, p. 296)

To be clear, our mental models make it possible to process large amounts of information quickly.

Mental Model Formation

The research states clearly that mental models are dynamic in nature because the human brain is constantly updating and refining its mental models. Thus, the literature often refers to mental models as *working* models. Mental models are formed as the result of the combination of (1) one's biology and (2) one's learning, which includes both experience and formal knowledge acquisition (e.g. graduate school or workplace training). Research has shown that mental models are particularly created during *analogical thinking* (i.e. when using analogies). Jones et al. (2011) explained analogical thinking the following way:

> When a person explains a domain with which they are unfamiliar, they tend to draw on a familiar domain, which they perceive as similar. This involves tapping into an existing mental model and importing its relational structure to another domain. For example, a mental model of water flow may be used to explain electric current; entities and relations corresponding to the former are mapped on to the model representing the latter. Experimental studies examining peoples' explanations of electricity … and water molecules … provide evidence in support of the idea that people do indeed use analogies in their cognitive processes. Analogical thinking allows people to "create new mental models that they can then run to generate predictions about what should happen in various situations in the real world" [quoting Collins & Gentner]. Mental models thus act as inferential frameworks ….
>
> (Jones et al., 2011, p. 2)

To be clear, learning means succeeding at inserting new information into an existing network of mental models. To learn is to adjust the original mental model to incorporate new information.

2 Learning is Minimizing Errors While Optimizing a Reward Function

While I will elaborate more on the benefit of mistakes in Chapter 2, the key here is to understand that the modification of one's mental model to *maximize accuracy* is a staple of adult learning. That is, adults are naturally wired to reduce the probability of committing an error or mistake (Dehaene, 2021).

3 Learning is Exploring the Space of Possibilities

As important as #2 is above, it is narrow-sighted to consider learning to be solely a function of reducing error. First, a lack of errors does not necessarily equate to arrival at an optimal solution. When attempting to minimize errors it is possible to overlook the best solution in favor of a lesser one that "gets the job done." As a result, exploration, curiosity, and even randomness play a critical role in adult learning because they allow for consideration of additional, potentially superior paths toward solution. For these reasons, a more complete view of learning is one that includes curiosity and randomness in the exploration of what is possible.

4 Learning is Inferring the Grammar of a Domain

It is a fundamental human characteristic to relentlessly seek abstract rules (i.e. high-level conclusions) that are extracted from one situation and then tested on an entirely new situation. Dehaene observed:

> Finding the appropriate law or logical rule that accounts for all available data is the ultimate means to massively accelerate learning—and the human brain is exceedingly good at this game ... Learning, in this sense, therefore means managing an internal hierarchy of rules and trying to infer, as soon as possible, the most general ones that summarize a whole series of observations. The human brain seems to apply this hierarchical principle from childhood.
>
> (Dehaene, 2021, pp. 35–36)

One specific area this principle is manifest in is learning the grammar of a domain. The acquisition of a domain's grammar more than simply learning words and phrases. Rather, grammar acquisition entails learning a domain's official vocabulary, short-hand terminology (i.e. slang or colloquialisms), and the appropriate uses of each. This process involves the identification of underlying rules and structures that define how concepts and relationships within a particular domain are represented and articulated. Learning such a distinction is also a hallmark of expert behavior, which I discuss further in the next chapter. The key takeaway here is that learning the grammar of a domain often occurs through inference, especially if the domain is related to the workplace. And inferential learning is a process that takes time.

Distinguishing Andragogy from Pedagogy

Having established a healthy conceptualization of what we mean by learning, I now shift to a discussion of the relationship between two important terms: *pedagogy* and *andragogy*. Pedagogy refers to the teaching of children or adolescents. Andragogy, conversely, is the study of teaching adults. While the focus of this book is exclusively andragogy (i.e. teaching adult learners), it is important to note that the two are not mutually exclusive; rather, it is better to think of pedagogy and andragogy as overlapping. Which raises the question: *Why make the distinction at all?*

Early in development, our nervous system is like a blank canvas, connected in very broad ways that make it difficult to do any one activity particularly well. From birth until around age 25 our neural connections are in development through the removal of connections that do not serve us well, or the strengthening of connections that relate to experiences which initially allow us to do things like walk, talk, read, etc. Then after age 25, if we want to change those neural connections that have formed the first 25 years of our life, we must engage in very intentional processes. Consequently, as adults you and I cannot simply "decide" to change our brain. We must first go through a series of steps that change our state, which then allows our brain to adapt and change (Huberman, 2021).

There are many things we know about how the developing brain learns that are shared with the already-developed adult brain. In this manner, some of the best practices for designing learning experiences for a develop*ing* brain are also best practices for a develop*ed* brain. Therefore, while the focus of this book is entirely on the adult brain (andragogy), it is important to know that many of the best practices for optimal adult learning are also best practices for children and/or adolescents. In short, please consider andragogy and pedagogy more as an overlapping Venn diagram and not as two diametrically opposed concepts.

Knowles's Assumptions

Related to andragogy, Dr. Malcolm Knowles (1980) proposed the following assumptions that are known as "Knowles's assumptions":

1 Adults become more self-directed as they mature.
2 An adult accumulates experience over time, which becomes a rich resource of their learning.
3 Adults want to know the reason for learning something, to always know "why."
4 The readiness of an adult to learn is closely related to the developmental tasks of his or her social role.
5 There is a change in time perspective as people mature—from future application of knowledge to immediacy of application. Thus, when it comes to learning, an adult is more problem-centered for immediate application, than subject-centered for future application.
6 Adults are mostly driven by internal motivation, rather than external motivators.

See also Hartree (1984) for a critique of Knowles.

Learning is Multidimensional

The next premise to establish is that adult learning consists of multiple dimensions simultaneously. The three primary dimensions of learning that scholars typically focus on are the *cognitive* (i.e. knowing), *behavioral* (i.e. doing), and *socio-emotional* (i.e. being, feeling, interacting). In the business and organizational behavior literature, this notion of multidimensionality is often represented by a person's KSAs, as defined previously. In organizational settings, it is important to understand that learning consists of improving or refining the combination of one's knowing, doing, and being so that the individual can perform at an optimal level in a given role. To that end, I will briefly consider each of these three dimensions as they provide a solid framework for the remainder of this book.

The *cognitive* aspects of learning are the central focus of Part II of this book. These chapters explore the neuroscientific principles most relevant to human learning, including the anatomy and physiology of our central nervous system (e.g. the brain, neurons, etc.), and key concepts such as memory and neuroplasticity. The *behavioral* dimension of adult learning is the heart of Part III. In isolation, the behavioral dimension of learning refers to the actions and motor skills that are learned through one's interaction with the external world. The *socio-emotional* dimension of learning is highlighted in Part IV. The socio-emotional dimension includes KSAs such as empathy, self-awareness, and collaboration, as well as attitude and mindset, each of which can either enhance or impede one's ability to learn and progress from novice to expert (Olszewski-Kubilius et al., 2016). The socio-emotional dimension also includes a person's ability to navigate interpersonal communication and relationships.

As you will see in the coming chapters, these three dimensions of learning do not exist in isolation; rather, they are interrelated. For example, if a person wanted to learn something highly behavioral like a physical or motor skill, such as improving the mechanics of their golf swing, there are still elements of learning involved that are quite cognitive. *Which golf club should I use in which situations? Where should my hands be at the top of the swing? If I wanted to hit a fade, where should my stance be versus where should my hands be at impact?* Each of these questions require one's cognition. So, you can see that even the highly behavioral activities require other dimensions for optimal learning and development. For

the purposes of instruction and clarity, I will explain these three dimensions individually in this book. However, as you proceed with your reading, please understand that the three dimensions are very much interrelated.

Transfer of Training

In workplace settings, the notion of a person applying what the person has learned to their job is often referred to in the scholarly literature as *transfer of training*. The idea here is that the individual "transfers" or applies the material they have learned in a training environment to their actual work environment. We will discuss the conditions of optimal transfer of training in a later chapter.

The Workplace

The workplace provides a unique setting in which learning occurs. It can consist of a physical, virtual, or hybrid (i.e. a combination of in-person and virtual) space. The workplace is composed of the people that inhabit it and the processes that link them. It also typically consists of an array of technological systems of varying capabilities that support the people and processes. The workplace also cannot be divorced from the organization that houses it. This includes the different levels of individual, team, and the organization as a whole. At each level there are goals, norms, and rules that guide and direct behaviors and decisions.

When discussing learning within the workplace (i.e. organizational contexts), we are referring to a setting that is much different than learning within a school. In fact, the workplace can refer to a number of different contexts and mini-cultures at once. On this exact point, Tynjälä (2008) argued that employees' status, background, role, and the organization's unique culture each influence one another and ultimately determine the way an employee will work and learn most effectively. The responsibility of the practitioner is to design learning experiences that allow enough versatility for employees from a range of backgrounds to be successful.

Workplace Learning

Jacobs and Park (2009) defined *workplace learning* as "the process by which individuals are engaged in training programs, education, development courses, or any type of learning activity for the purpose of acquiring the competence necessary to meet current and future work requirements" (p. 134). Under this umbrella, Tynjälä (2008) observed four aspects of workplace learning that are important to review:

1. Workplace learning (WL) is both similar to and different from learning in a school setting.
2. WL exists at multiple levels: individual, team, organization, community, and region.
3. WL occurs through both informal and formal means.
4. There is a spectrum in the amount of WL support that is offered by different organizations. Some offer their employees a great deal of WL support; some do not.

Application of This Chapter

In most of the chapters that follow, I include a section devoted to answering the questions, *So what? What should be the take-aways of this chapter that I can apply to my organizational*

Table 1.1 Formal education versus workplace learning.

Learning in formal education settings	*Workplace learning*
Individual	Often collaborative
Largely intentional, with some unintentional	Largely unintentional, with some intentional
Prescribed by formal curriculum, standards, etc.	Minimal formal curriculum or prescribed outcomes
Focus on mental activities	Focus on tool use and mental activities
Theory and practice traditionally separated	Know-how usually connected to practical application

Source: Synthesized from Tynjälä (2008)

context? However, the purpose of this first chapter was to provide a foundational overview of the various subfields, concepts, and terms related to adult learning, particularly within the workplace. So while this chapter is less directly applicable compared to the remining chapters, the absence of a specific example of application (i.e. one not tailored to a specific industry, function, situation, etc.) does not dilute the importance of what is being discussed. In fact, in my experience we can nearly always use learning science to navigate an organizational landscape. In my view, that is a very tactical notion.

References

Chen, G., & Klimoski, R. J. (2007). Training and development of human resources at work: Is the state of our science strong?. *Human Resource Management Review*, 17(2), 180–190.

Dachner, A. M., Ellingson, J. E., Noe, R. A., & Saxton, B. M. (2021). The future of employee development. *Human Resource Management Review*, 31(2), 100732.

Dehaene, S. (2021). *How we learn: Why brains learn better than any machine ... for now*. Penguin.

DeSimone, R.L., Werner, J.M., & Harris, D.M. (2002). *Human resource development* (3rd ed.). Harcourt.

Eren, M. E. (2014). Performance increasing of the Dusseldorf Turkish general consulate. *International Journal of Human Sciences*, 11(2), 1062.

Ericsson, A., & Pool, R. (2016). *Peak: Secrets from the new science of expertise*. Random House.

Farrington-Darby, T., & Wilson, J. R. (2006). The nature of expertise: A review. *Applied Ergonomics*, 37(1), 17–32.

Fischbein, E., Tirosh, D., Stavy, R., & Oster, A. (1990). The autonomy of mental models. *For the learning of mathematics*, 10(1), 23–30.

Hameed, A., & Waheed, A. (2011). Employee development and its affect on employee performance a conceptual framework. *International Journal of Business and Social Science*, 2(13).

Hartree, A. (1984). Malcolm Knowles' theory of andragogy: A critique. *International Journal of Lifelong Education*, 3(3), 203–210. doi:10.1080/0260137840030304.

Huberman, A. (Producer). (2021). How your brain works & changes [video podcast]. www.hubermanlab.com/episode/how-your-nervoussystem-works-and-changes.

Jacob, E. K., & Shaw, D. (1998). Sociocognitive perspectives on representation. *Annual Review of Information Science and Technology (ARIST)*, 33, 131–185.

Jacobs, R. L., & Park, Y. (2009). A proposed conceptual framework of workplace learning: Implications for theory development and research in human resource development. *Human Resource Development Review*, 8(2), 133–150.

Jones, N. A., Ross, H., Lynam, T., Perez, P., & Leitch, A. (2011). Mental models: An interdisciplinary synthesis of theory and methods. *Ecology and Society*, 16(1).

Klovienė, L. and Uosytė, I. (2019). Development of performance measurement system in the context of industry 4: A case study. *Engineering Economics*, 30(4), 472–482.

Knowles, M. S. (1980). From pedagogy to andragogy. *Religious Education*, 75(4), 202–211.

Lee, C. H., & Bruvold, N. T. (2003). Creating value for employees: Investment in employee development. *The International Journal of Human Resource Management*, 14(6), 981–1000.

Mathieu, J. E., Heffner, T. S., Goodwin, G. F., Salas, E., & Cannon-Bowers, J. A. (2000). The influence of shared mental models on team process and performance. *Journal of Applied Psychology*, 85(2), 273.

Olszewski-Kubilius, P., Subotnik, R. F., & Worrell, F. C. (2016). The role of domains in the conceptualization of talent. In D. Ambrose & R. J. Sternberg (Eds.), *Giftedness and talent in the 21st century* (pp. 81–99). Brill.

Rummler, G. A., & Brache, A. (1992). Transforming organizations through human performance technology. In H. D. Stolovich & E. J. Keeps (Eds.), *Handbook of human performance technology: A comprehensive guide for analyzing and solving performance problems in organizations* (pp. 32–49). Jossey-Bass.

Swanson, R. A. (1999). The foundations of performance improvement and implications for practice. In R. Torraco (Ed.), *The theory and practice of performance improvement* (pp. 1–25). Berrett-Koehler.

Sweller, J. (1994). Cognitive load theory, learning difficulty, and instructional design. *Learning and Instruction*, 4(4), 295–312.

Tynjälä, P. (2008). Perspectives into learning at the workplace. *Educational Research Review*, 3(2), 130–154.

Wang, G. G., Werner, J. M., Sun, J. Y., Gilley, A., & Gilley, J. W. (2017). Means vs ends: Theorizing a definition of human resource development. *Personnel Review*, 46(6), 1165–1181.

Yadav, N., Shankar, R., & Singh, S. P. (2020). Impact of industry4.0, lean six sigma, and quality management systems on organizational performance. *The TQM Journal*, 32(4), 815–835.

2 Developing Expertise

As adult learning and development (L&D) professionals and scholars, we are most interested in the science and practice developing novices into experts. As such, it is imperative that we be familiar with the research and principles of expertise and how to develop it most effectively. This chapter provides you with an overview of the advancements made in psychological research surrounding expertise development, as well as practical ways to apply the principles of expertise development to your own workplace.

The Real Top Gun

Who do you think of when you picture an expert? For me, one of my favorite fictional characters comes to mind. You have probably heard of or seen the *Top Gun* movies. As far as entertainment is concerned, Maverick is one of my favorite characters in all of cinema. As a child, I wanted to be "Mav" so much, defeating the enemy in dogfight combat. To this day, I still get a kick out of a good aerial combat movie. Yet when you strip away the glamour and drama shown to us from Hollywood, the real Top Gun is still quite impressive. In fact, the real Top Gun is a strong example of a training program that successfully used—and still uses to this day—the principles covered in this chapter.

The year was 1968 and the U.S. was in the middle of the Vietnam War. During the previous years from 1965 through 1967, U.S. pilots had won two out of every three dogfights against North Vietnamese fighters (Chatham, 2009). But the Vietnamese began using Russian-made MiG jets and by early 1968, the win ratio dropped to 1-to-1. In other words, for every enemy shot down, the U.S. lost one of its own pilots as well, which was a terrible ratio for the U.S. The senior leaders of the U.S. Navy knew changes needed to be made, so they formally assessed the situation. Not surprisingly, the Navy's assessment of the pilots' preparedness was scathing. One of its many recommendations was to establish a dedicated, advanced training school exclusively for fighter pilots.

So later in 1968, naval senior leaders formed the U.S. Navy Fighter Weapons School, which today is officially the U.S. Navy Strike Fighter Tactics Instructor Program. ("Top Gun" is the affectionate nickname for the school.) The mission of the Fighter Weapons School was simple: to improve the U.S. pilots' kill ratio. The first order of business was to select the best, most-successful pilots and appoint them as instructors. The students invited to attend the school as participants were the next best pilots. The daily training was very similar to what is depicted in the movies. In the mornings, the student pilots would fight against the instructor pilots (who played the role of the enemy) in a variety of different combat situations, using cameras and lasers in place of live bullets and missiles. This approach provided pilots with the opportunity to try different things and make mistakes without the fatal consequences of a real dogfight.

DOI: 10.4324/9781003593607-3

In the afternoon, the students and instructors attended classroom sessions for evaluation and coaching, known as "after-action reports." In these sessions, the instructors would ask: "Why did you do X? What were you thinking here? What might you have done differently?" After the questioning, the instructors would always offer recommendations and coaching points so the students could consider alternative and better ways to handle the situation. They would then repeat this process each day.

The results of this training were extraordinary. From 1970 to 1973, U.S. pilots shot down Vietnamese fighters at approximately a 12-to-1 ratio. Based on this success, the U.S. Air Force adopted a very similar approach into its own pilot training program. The U.S. Armed Forces have continued refining the training of pilots ever since. Many years later, by the time the First Gulf War came around in the early 1990s, U.S. pilots shot down enemy pilots at the staggering rate of 33-to-1. Clearly, Top Gun was doing something very right—but why was this the case?

Top Gun succeeded because it brought in top performers of the field to train other, lesser performers to bring them closer to the top level. Additionally, despite heavy debate among the program creators on how hard to push the pilots, the pilots learned best when they were pushed out of their comfort zones. In doing so, they were able to make mistakes without the costs associated with actual combat warfare. Lastly, Top Gun also succeeded because it emphasized *doing*. The deliberate practice at the school focused largely on performance (i.e. doing) and how to improve it. For our purposes, the significance here is that the pilots were able to combine the *knowing* with the *doing*, with the emphasis on the *doing*.

Table 2.1 Elements of the Top Gun program that led to developing combat expertise.

"Top Gun" application	*Principle of developing expertise*
Employed the most skilled and successful fighter pilots (i.e. experts) as instructors, who shared their insight with students.	Access to the mental models of expert performers.
During the "after-action reports," the instructors (i.e. experts) provided immediate feedback and suggested alternative approaches.	Access to strong, quality feedback.
Real, in-the-sky dogfighting with instructors, mimicking a wide variety of combat situations.	Purposeful, deliberate practice.
Student pilots were pushed beyond their comfort zones, but in an environment where they could make mistakes without the consequences of actual warfare.	A healthy level of difficulty as part of that practice (i.e. not too easy, not impossibly difficult).

The Nature of Expertise

The Top Gun example is an illustration of the principles involved in developing expertise. To begin, let us first consider the question, *what is expertise?*

> Expertise involves the acquisition, storage, and utilization of at least two kinds of knowledge: explicit knowledge of a domain and implicit or tacit knowledge of a field … where *domain* refers to a knowledge base, and *field* to the social organization of that knowledge base …
>
> (Sternberg, 1998, p. 13)

Novice ⟷ Competent ⟷ Expert ⟷ Eminent

Figure 2.1 Expertise continuum

Explicit knowledge is the most frequently cited in the literature, and consists of knowledge concerning facts, formulas, principles, procedures, and major ideas of a domain that can be consciously recalled at will. For example, you may know the steps to successfully bake a cake, or who invented the lightbulb. *Implicit,* or "tacit," knowledge refers to the unconscious awareness of how to complete certain tasks and activities without the need to consciously recall that information, such as riding a bicycle.

Building on this early definition, one of the foremost scholars on expertise development, psychology professor Dr. Anders Ericsson, said this:

> Real expertise must pass three tests. First, it must lead to performance that is consistently superior to that of the expert's peers. Second, real expertise produces concrete results. Brain surgeons, for example, not only must be skillful with their scalpels but also must have successful outcomes with their patients. A chess player must be able to win matches in tournaments. Finally, true expertise can be replicated and measured in the lab. As the British scientist Lord Kelvin stated, "If you cannot measure it, you cannot improve it."
>
> (Ericsson et al., 2007, para. 8)

While Figure 2.1 may appear linear, the development of expertise is a dynamic and fluid process and is therefore best represented as a complex continuum. An individual's place on that continuum (i.e. the aggregate of their current KSA levels) is simply a reflection of their expertise that is in-development at the current moment. It is therefore a snapshot, and as such does not tell the entire story. "Individuals are constantly in a process of developing expertise when they work within a given domain. They may and do, of course, differ in rate and asymptote of development" (Sternberg, 1998, p. 16). Csikszentmihalyi et al. (2018) described expertise–which is sometimes also referred to as *talent* or *giftedness*, depending on the context–as a dynamic quality that depends on changes within an individual, changes within the environment, and the relationship between the two.

Nevertheless, for our discussion it can be useful to talk about the development of expertise as a progression, from novice to eminence. Table 2.2 unpacks the characteristics of each level.

Table 2.2 Levels of expertise.

Level	*Characteristics*
Novice	Novices are relatively new to a particular field or domain. As such, their KSAs (knowledge, skills, abilities) are underdeveloped.
Competent	Competent individuals have a good grasp of the basic principles and practices of their domain and can apply them in routine situations.
Expert	Experts possess very high levels of competence. They can handle complex and novel situations with ease, often relying on a blend of intuition (sometimes called a "hunch") and analytical thinking (sustained, systematic thought).
Eminent	Eminence is the pinnacle of expertise, going beyond individual mastery to making significant, lasting contributions to a field. This is the "hall of fame" level, as those who achieve eminence are often sought after for their insights and top performance among other experts.

Novice

Historically, individual differences in ability were seen as a result of genetic endowment (i.e. people having a fixed potential for achievement). But we now know this is very much not the case. That is, KSAs are not set in stone and can be improved and developed over time.

> Abilities are seen as themselves a form of developing expertise. An important educational implication of this view is that abilities, like expertise, can be taught. (Abilities) are seen as modifiable in some degree and as capable of being flexibly implemented at the same time that they are viewed as having interactive genetic and environmental components.
>
> (Sternberg, 1998, p. 11)

The key idea here is that the KSAs of novices are entirely underdeveloped.

Competent

As a person succeeds in developing an expertise, various factors play important roles.

> In the course of transition from novice to expert and beyond, key personality, ability, and skill factors become increasingly or decreasingly important. In accordance with these premises, we believe that abilities have interactive genetic and environmental components, yet are modifiable and capable of being flexibly deployed.
>
> (Subotnik & Jarvin, 2005, p. 343)

Internal abilities refer to things like intrinsic motivation and charisma. When taken together, however, "The best evidence favors a complex mix of genetic and environmental origins of abilities, interacting in ways that are not as yet fully known" (Sternberg & Grigorenko, 1997).

The effectiveness of a person's growth from novice toward greater competence is mediated by several factors: the rate of learning; support (or, conversely, pressure); the person's teachability; the quality of the learner-teacher interactions; the availability of external rewards such as praise and recognition; and persistence through good and bad times.

Expert

Being an expert means possessing mastery or, in other words, high levels of competence. Comparing an expert to a novice is a simple way to distinguish what an expert is. Table 2.3 below provides a clear delineation between the two. This interpretation forms the foundation for two related types of reasoning used by experts: ***analysis*** and ***intuition***. Analysis involves sustained, systematic thought over a substantial span of time (minutes to hours), while intuition reflects timely, and seemingly less deliberate, reasoning that is sometimes referred to as a hunch or professional judgment.

Analytical Reasoning

The depth of analytical reasoning for an expert is relatively much greater, and broader, when compared to that of a novice. The expert's level of analytical reasoning is typically associated with complex problem solving. It consists of gathering information, mobilizing relevant knowledge, making observations about the situation, and proposing solutions. For

Table 2.3 Juxtaposition of novices and experts across eight dimensions.

	Novice	*Expert*
Range of perspective	A narrower gaze. Cannot see the big picture; focused on the immediate view (i.e. on the details).	A broader gaze. Can simultaneously see the big picture and the details at the same time.
Depth of knowledge base	Limited knowledge base.	Extensive, current content knowledge base. Less cognitive effort required to draw upon that knowledge.
Social intelligence	Lack of refined socio-emotional skills.	Advanced ability to control motivation, cope with stress, openness to feedback, growth mindset.
Pattern recognition	Can only perceive smaller patterns in their domain.	Strong recognition of patterns and features. Better at identifying and adapting to exceptions.
Self-awareness	Awareness of cognitive difficulties.	Greater skill in anticipation, prediction, and in drawing inferences. Greater awareness of one's own capacity.
How problems are conceptualized	Represents a problem at a superficial level; generates a more-narrow solution.	Represents a problem at a deeper level; chooses better strategies to solve, generates solutions with higher accuracy (metacognition*)
How problems are solved	Requires deliberate, intentional thought to solve problems.	Many sequences of steps within problem solving are automatized.
Response to novel situations	Flustered, uncomfortable under the stress of being in a situation that is new or for which they are unprepared.	Calm when presented with a situation they have not encountered before. Poise under pressure.

*Metacognition refers to people's understanding and control of their own cognition. It includes both the steps involved, and how the steps can be executed effectively.

example, a chess master may ponder many moves before actually selecting one. Or, a doctor may request various tests before settling on a diagnosis. A manager may review several analytical reports before making a decision. Even for experts, analytical reasoning takes time and requires extensive use of mental capital. Yet the key is that the time and mental capital required for an expert is much less than that of a novice, and this leads to the next aspect of expert behavior.

Intuitive Reasoning

At times, experts generate accurate solutions without thinking more than a few seconds and without appearing to examine the situation ultra-closely. Using one's intuition can be somewhat of a leap, and the person taking the leap is often not aware of how he or she did it. In this sense, generating solutions for problems becomes *automatic* as expertise grows. (I will discuss the phenomenon of "schema automation" in greater detail later in this book.)

How does intuition work? Extensive experience leads to the emergence of patterns. Over time, individuals begin to recognize these patterns in similar situations, such that familiar patterns immediately suggest a possible move, a possible condition, a possible cause (e.g. when troubleshooting), or a possible risk. Such associations evolve over time and persist

because they contribute to success in future problem solving. Intuitive reasoning, therefore, is based on an understanding that an expert hones over an extended period. Eventually, what once called for analytical steps then evolves into intuition.

The ability to generate intuitive responses does not of course mean we are beholden to those decisions. For example, from a quick look at a test result, the radiologist can offer an initial hypothesis about what is going on, but may still choose to review the patient's chart, consult a colleague, and/or run more tests. The corporate executive may have a "gut feel" for the causes of a certain situation, but proceeds to confirm or refute intuition through more impartial analysis. So whether it be in a laboratory setting or in real-world practice, expert analysis and intuition merge to produce expert performance.

To illustrate, the internet is full of stories of consultants or contract workers who perform a quality job in a shorter amount of time than the full scope, but still charged full price. Naturally, the client does not want to pay full price of it taking longer. The consultant then tells the client that the full price essentially covers the graduate degree and years of experience that gave the consultant the KSAs necessary to perform such a quality job in a shorter amount of time in the first place.

Dunning–Kruger Effect

In a discussion of expert performance and what distinguishes experts from the rest, we should also consider the psychological phenomenon known as the *Dunning–Kruger effect*. This effect occurs when a person overestimates their own abilities due to a lack of knowledge and skill in the field (i.e. the individual does not know how much they do not know) (Kruger & Dunning, 1999). As their skills improve and the person gains more experience, they become increasingly aware of the complexities and intricacies of the work involved and are then able to put their expertise into perspective. In fact, some of the greatest experts in their fields can underestimate their own abilities to the extent they fail to recognize how far they have come in relation to others.

Whether it is the Dunning-Kruger effect or any other cognitive bias, what is of importance to us is recognizing and acknowledging that cognitive biases exist, especially when it comes to creating effective and targeted learning experiences to address specific gaps in KSAs.

Eminent

Beyond expert performance is the rarified air of being the best-of-the-best, known in the psychological literature as *eminence*. Eminence refers to a level of superior expertise and achievement even among other experts (Baker et al., 2019). External indicators of eminence typically include career length, or awards such as MVP (most valuable player/person) and Hall of Fame. Simonton (1977) discovered "that both creative productivity and creative longevity were indeed direct predictors of eminence in that domain" (p. 16). Further, eminence may even extend beyond one's area of expertise, involving broader recognition and appreciation of their contributions to society, their ability to inspire others, and the individual's overall influence on a larger scale.

What attributes typically accompany eminence? Subotnik et al. (2011) answered this question: "Several researchers argue that motivation, drive, and grit are at the center of eminent levels of achievement … and credit motivation with determining an individual's ability to garner, respond to, and capitalize on talent development opportunities" (p. 17).

Additionally, an individual's high passion for the domain is also a hallmark of eminence (Bonneville-Roussy & Vallerand, 2020).

Developing Expertise

To develop expertise of any type or in any domain, research from the field of psychology has revealed four fundamental elements that must be present over sustained time:

1 Access to the mental models of expert (or top) performers.
2 Access to strong, timely feedback.
3 Purposeful, deliberate practice (which is a specific type of practice).
4 A desirable level of difficulty as a part of that practice.

For the remainder of this chapter, I will discuss each of the four elements.

Access to Expert Mental Models

Recall from Chapter 1 that mental models provide the framework from which individuals interpret, make sense of, understand, and anticipate the world around them (Westbrook, 2006). Mental models are what provide individuals the capacity to reason as well as determine the causality (i.e. the cause-and-effect) of a phenomenon (Jones et al., 2011). In this manner, the mental models of top performers (or experts) are what allow them to make faster, more accurate decisions and respond more quickly and effectively in a given situation. It is this ability to tap into advanced mental models, beyond anything else, that accounts for the difference in performance between novices and experts. In short, while the mental models of novices are relatively incomplete, and/or inaccurate, bringing with them varying levels of effectiveness, by comparison the mental models of experts are more developed, more nuanced, and more accurate.

Ultimately, what sets experts apart from the rest of us is that their years of experience and/or practice have changed the neural circuitry in their brains to produce highly specialized mental models, which in turn make possible the incredible memory, pattern recognition, problem solving, and other advanced abilities needed to excel in their specialties. Highly developed mental processes are seen in expert performers in every field and hold the key to understanding their extraordinary ability. For example, expert chess players can look at a board in the middle of a game and be able to recall the layout of the board almost perfectly afterward - something that defies what is known regarding the limits of short-term memory.

As a result, as far as developing expertise is concerned, we are interested in studying the top performers precisely because they are the possessors of the top mental models. One advantage of accessing the top mental models stems from being able to see the details and the bigger picture at the same time (see the top row of Table 2.3). In other words, top mental representations allow a person to see the forest and the trees simultaneously, as needed. For example, in chess that means seeing (1) the pieces, (2) the interactions between them, (3) the strength and weaknesses of both players' positions, and (4) the moves that are likely to be effective in such positions. Research has shown that what sets grandmaster chess players apart from novice or midrange chess players is their ability to devise much better potential moves when examining a position (Hearst & Knott, 2009; De Groot, 2014). Specifically, these representations allow a chess master to zero in on individual pieces and mentally move them around the board to see how such moves would change the patterns. Similarly, I research leader development and the same processes work for expert leaders when compared to novice leaders: the experts have more advanced mental models of various situations and the optimal decisions to make when confronted

with those situations. Such expert leader mental models are typically the result of the combination of experience, training, and coaching.

In general, what sets experts apart from everyone else is the *quality*, *quantity*, and *integration* of their mental models. The expert's advantage lies in their ability to envision more possible outcomes and quickly sift through them and arrive at the most promising action. They possess a more developed ability to interpret the pattern of action on the field. In short, more developed, more robust mental representations lead to better performance.

The more a person knows a field, domain, or sport, and the more they study it, (1) the more detailed the mental models become, and (2) the better the person gets at assimilating new information. For example, studies show that expert physicians distinguish themselves from the other physicians by their ability to generate a number of likely diagnoses and carefully reason through them (see Monteiro & Norman, 2013; Patel et al., 1994; Johnson et al., 1981). When an actual surgery diverges from a surgeon's mental representation (i.e. presented with a novel situation), expert surgeons know to slow down, rethink options, and if necessary, formulate a new plan in response to the new information (see bottom row of Table 2.3). Research has also demonstrated that expert sales agents possessed much more complex and integrated mental representations than less successful agents (Leigh et al., 2014). Specifically, the research showed the expert sales agents had developed advanced "If ... then ..." structures (e.g., "If [condition], then [action taken]"), so they knew what to do more quickly and more accurately in any given situation, ultimately making them more effective agents. This superior organization of information in long-term memory is a consistent theme when studying expert performers.

In terms of metacognition (i.e. the awareness of and ability to manage one's own thinking), expert performers use mental models to improve their own performance by monitoring and evaluating their performance and, when necessary, modifying their mental models to update them or make them more effective. Thus, the value of expert/top performers is to provide access to the mental representations that produce their top performance.

Types of Mental Models

Cognitive mental models, behavioral mental models, and socio-emotional mental models represent distinct frameworks through which individuals understand and interact with the world. Each of these models serves a unique purpose and reflects different dimensions of human cognition and experience. Understanding these distinctions enables a comprehensive approach to learning, adapting interventions, and fostering personal development in both educational and organizational contexts:

- **Cognitive mental models** are fundamentally concerned with how individuals mentally represent knowledge and understanding. These models help people to process information and conceptually organize their experiences, which in turn help individuals synthesize information, make decisions, and solve problems. These mental representations allow learners to map relationships between different concepts, frameworks, or processes, enabling predictions and informed decision-making based on their understanding of the underlying dynamics within a domain (Dong et al., 2022). For example, cognitive maps are a form of cognitive mental model that individuals use to navigate and understand spatial relationships in their environment.
- **Behavioral mental models** focus on observable actions and the rationale behind these actions. These models particularly concern themselves with understanding how external stimuli influence behavior. For example, Fogg's (2019) behavioral model identifies key

factors that drive behavior—motivation, ability, and prompts. This model is especially relevant in fields such as marketing and behavior modification, where understanding what triggers specific actions can lead to more effective interventions. Behavioral models concentrate on predicting and shaping behavior based on situational inputs, thereby providing clarity in designing systems and environments that influence human actions (Fogg, 2019).

- **Socio-emotional mental models** pertain to the emotional and social constructs that shape interactions between individuals. These models encapsulate the emotional responses and social dynamics that influence behavior and decision-making within social contexts. For instance, research by Farrant et al. (2010) highlighted the importance of socio-emotional engagement in the development of communication skills, indicating that emotional and social factors underpin cognitive development. Socio-emotional mental models are particularly relevant in education and therapeutic settings where fostering emotional intelligence and social skills is critical for personal development and interpersonal relationships.

The interaction between these three types of mental models is significant. For example, a person's cognitive understanding of a situation may dictate their behavioral response, which is further influenced by emotional states and social contexts. The integration of cognitive and behavioral models informs socio-emotional responses as well, as individuals might leverage their cognitive understanding of social cues to determine their emotional reactions.

Providing Access to Expert Mental Models

For professionals interested in developing expertise within their ranks, to provide access to top mental representations please consider these points below.

1 It is not necessary for the top performers to be the teachers/coaches themselves. In the Top Gun example, the top performers and the teachers were one and the same; however, this does not have to be the case. For instance, in many sports the most effective coaches were not top players themselves.
2 How are you ensuring that the learning experience being designed relies on the mental representations of the expert/top performers, and not lesser mental representations of mediocre performers?
3 Are you seeking those who have done an elite job themselves, or even scholars who have researched top performance? Or, are you settling for convenience (like LinkedIn trends)?
4 What books or articles are you referring to? And why? Are the podcasts or videos from which you seek information based on interviews of experts?

To conclude this section, Nersessian (2002, p. 140) stated, "The nature and richness of models one can construct and one's ability to reason develops with learning domain-specific content and techniques."

Access to Strong, Timely Feedback

For optimal expertise development, the research shows that it is more critical that strong feedback be provided in the first place, regardless of source. What does the scholarly literature mean by good, strong feedback? Unfortunately, the scholarly literature indicates

mixed results. First, the research reveals a large variability of effects from feedback. In fact, Kluger and DeNisi (1996) famously meta-analyzed nearly a century's worth of research on feedback and found "a large variability of feedback intervention effects such that in over one third of the cases feedback interventions *reduced* performance" (p. 275, emphasis added). As a result of their meta-analysis, Kluger and DeNisi concluded that feedback can easily be characterized as a double-edged sword "because feedback interventions do not always increase performance and under certain conditions are detrimental to performance" (p. 275).

With that premise, what does the literature describe as the right conditions for feedback to improve performance? Fortunately, for this question the research is more definitive and clear. First, feedback effectiveness is moderated by one's focus of attention—the more the attention of the feedback is placed on the *task* and not the *self*, the better (Kluger & DeNisi, 1996). To be crystal clear, the research does not center on the feedback giver's locus of attention; rather, it is the locus of attention of the feedback receiver that has the moderating effect of feedback effectiveness. The data show that the greater the feedback receiver's attention is centered on the task and not himself or herself, the more effective the feedback is at improving performance. Therefore, it behooves the feedback provider to make it as simple as possible for the receiver to focus on the task, and not on himself or herself.

Second, the research on effective feedback delivery is quite straightforward: strong feedback consists of an immediate and clear articulation of the (1) desired state, (2) current state, and (3) the path for how to get from current to desired (i.e. how to traverse the performance gap). Research has shown that becoming aware of the difference between these two states (i.e. desired state vs. current state) engages the receiver's brain systems that drive attention, effort, and persistence in pursuit of a goal. Note that research suggests that strong feedback be *immediate*, meaning there is minimal delay between an action and the corresponding feedback for the recipient. Research has proven that feedback that is both immediate and clear is of the most benefit to the recipient (Wisniewski et al., 2020).

I stated above that the source of feedback is of secondary importance, but the question remains: from where does strong feedback most often come? A quality coach, teacher, or leader is one who typically offers strong feedback that an individual could not receive any other way. In fact, Olszewski-Kubilius et al. (2016) observed, "The talent development process is driven by expert teachers, mentors, and coaches who provide opportunities for gaining knowledge and honing skills" (p. 64). Additionally, "Great teachers encourage their students to embrace rather than fear adversity, as mastery over such fear allows for persistence through practice, disappointment, and even failure" (Subotnik & Jarvin, 2005, p. 344).

In the Top Gun example, it just so happened that the top performers were also the teachers—they were one in the same. But this does not have to be the case; in fact, it is often not. For instance, in the sport of golf the best coaches are almost always people who were not top players themselves. Why is this the case? Because being a top performer is by no means a requirement to providing strong, effective feedback.

Thus, the importance of strong feedback places emphasis on the role of a coach, teacher, or leader. That person must draw from a highly developed body of knowledge and determine the best way to teach skills. A good teacher empowers you and provides valuable feedback you could not receive any other way. Effective feedback is much more than right and wrong; it is about helping the learner understand the mental models needed to succeed. So, a highly effective coach/teacher/leader is one who offers advice on how to think more effectively about the problem at hand in a manner that bridges the past KSA to the ideal KSA (Ericsson & Poole, 2016).

Deliberate Practice

The third key to developing expertise is to engage in purposeful, deliberate practice—in other words, it involves *doing the thing*. The emphasis here is on *doing*. The main objective of purposeful, deliberate practice is to develop effective mental representations, and this is accomplished by challenging homeostasis. *Homeostasis* is a biological term which refers to the human body's self-regulating mechanism by which it maintains internal stability and consistency while adjusting to changing external conditions. For example, using homeostasis to drive physical change, if we push our body hard enough for long enough (e.g. lifting weights over an extended period of time), the body will respond by changing in ways that make subsequent pushes easier to do. Similarly, the brain, like the body, changes when pushed outside—but not too far outside—of its comfort zone. We know this is what occurs through research:

> Deliberate practice is different. It entails considerable, specific, and sustained efforts to do something you can't do well—or even at all. Research across domains shows that it is only by working at what you can't do that you turn into the expert you want to become.
>
> (Ericsson et al., 2007)

To be clear, experience alone does not improve performance. In fact, based on research done on physicians, physician performance actually grew *worse* over time, or at best remained the same. One thing is clear from research, neither doctors nor nurses necessarily gain expertise from experience alone. In research on different educational interventions for physicians, they found the most effective interventions contained an interactive component–roleplay, discussion groups, case solving, hands-on training, and the like (see Pusic et al., 2011; Choudhry et al., 2005; Lesgold et al., 2014). Thus, for physicians deliberate practice is greater than experience alone.

Why is this the case? The conclusion was that attending lectures, mini courses, and the like offers little to no feedback and little opportunity to try something new, make mistakes, correct the mistakes, and gradually develop a new skill. The key question is: *how do we improve relevant skills?* Rather than, how do we teach the relevant knowledge? As we saw from the Top Gun example, training should focus on *doing* rather than *knowing*.

From studying musicians, we know that long-term training results in changes in those parts of the brain that are relevant to the particular skill being developed (Kawabata, 2007; Grape et al., 2002; Lehmann & Ericsson, 1998). While details vary from skill to skill, the overall pattern is consistent: deliberate practice leads to changes in the parts of the brain that are challenged by the practice (Ericsson & Faivre, 1988). The brain adapts to these challenges by rewiring itself in ways that increase its ability to carry out the functions required by the challenges–a process known as *neuroplasticity*. We will discuss neuroplasticity in more detail in Chapters 4 and 5.

The Process of Purposeful, Deliberate Practice

The first task to develop any KSA is to break it down into its constituent parts. Then, the best way to improve the expertise is through focused, deliberate practice of those parts, one at a time. To illustrate, let us look at the US Navy SEAL's, who must learn a variety of skills: combat, survival, medical, swimming/diving, cultures, and sometimes a new language. To accomplish learning these skills, their training consists of first determining the overall objective and then immediately breaking it down into smaller pieces, mastering one

piece at a time. They do this until they can put multiple smaller pieces together and accomplish higher-order tasks. They repeat this as needed until the final objective is achieved.

Further, deliberate practice should be informed and guided by (1) the top performers' mental models and (2) what those experts do to excel. Deliberate practice is defined by a number of features (Ericsson & Poole, 2016):

- Deliberate practice is purposeful, requiring a person's undivided attention, focus, and concentration.
- Deliberate practice relies on effective mental representations; it also produces effective mental representations. In this manner deliberate practice is cyclical: honing a skill improves the mental representation, and the mental representation helps hone the skill.
- Deliberate practice centers on highly-specific goals.
- Deliberate practice relies on feedback (see the previous section above).

A Desirable Level of Difficulty

The fourth pillar for optimal expertise development is the presence of a desirable level of difficulty or challenge. To be clear, both resistance and mistakes are required for growth, development, and neuroplasticity to be possible. Let me repeat that: both resistance and mistakes are necessary ingredients to achieve optimal growth, development, and neuroplasticity. There is a term in the L&D world affectionately referred to as ***desirable difficulty***—the idea being that there is a range of healthy challenge that is optimal for learning (i.e. desirable), and anything outside of that range is therefore suboptimal for learning (i.e. undesirable). Let us unpack the ***desirable difficulty*** phenomenon further.

Resistance

Research shows that an appropriate level of difficulty, challenge, or resistance is required to stimulate the attention and engagement of the learner (Bjork & Bjork, 2011, 2020). To use a fitness analogy, imagine a very strong weightlifter. Did he or she become strong by lifting very light weights? Of course not. It is no secret that to increase in physical strength we must continually add weight and repetitions to our lifts. The continual push is necessary. Now conversely, consider a very skinny, non-muscular person. How strong might this person expect to get by only lifting a pencil (or something light)? No chance. Therefore, embedded in the attempt to increase in physical strength is the necessity of an optimal range of resistance to challenge the muscles over time.

The same principle holds for developing expertise. Regarding this exact point, Bjork and Bjork (2011) stated, "Desirable difficulties are desirable because they trigger encoding and retrieval processes that support learning, comprehension, and remembering. If, however, the learner does not have the background knowledge or skills to respond to them successfully, they become undesirable difficulties" (p. 58). To put it simply, too much of a challenge would be counterproductive because repeated failures is not helpful; and too little resistance is also counterproductive because it would lead to atrophy and/or boredom. Thus, the sweet spot of a desirable difficulty is a challenge that is neither too easy nor too hard.

Mistakes and Errors

Making mistakes is *beneficial* for neuroplasticity. Whenever a person tries to learn something new, it is not uncommon for them to naturally struggle at first, make mistakes, and

while this can be frustrating, it is necessary for figuring out how to do things correctly. However, the recognition of the mistake and the state of frustration actually cue-up particular brain areas to be more alert so that on subsequent attempts they can better learn the correct KSA. This is why persistence and grit are vitally important moderators in developing expertise.

First, learning is affected by our attitude and response toward the mistake. By not acknowledging a mistake, a person becomes less able to cope with error or even failure, which negatively impacts the potential for learning (Danielmeier & Ullsperger, 2011). Conversely, learning becomes more possible if mistakes are embraced and viewed as a challenge. When a person does something incorrectly, their brain releases neurochemicals (i.e. epinephrine and acetylcholine, which I will discuss further in Chapter 5) that increases their attention and awareness. Then if the person does the task correctly, their brain will release dopamine, which increases the feeling of happiness about what has been accomplished and in turn increases motivation, which ultimately serves to enhance learning.

THE 85/15 RULE

A professional should seek to create a challenging learning objective, but not so lofty that achieving it is unattainable. Ideally, the brain likes difficult tasks, but not so hard as to cause discouragement or high anxiety. The adult brain wants enough of a challenge/difficulty so as to generate arousal and focus, and therefore, neuroplasticity. In highly referenced research, Wilson et al. (2019) found the ratio of 85% correct to 15% errors to be the "sweet spot" where an individual's learning progresses most efficiently and quickly. How did they determine this? Wilson et al. tested for optimal error rate over time across three cases. In cases one and two, the authors conducted two machine learning simulations using one- and two-layer neural networks. In case three, they relied on a computational neuroscience model that describes human and animal perceptual learning. (Specifically, it was the *Law and Gold model*, which accounts for the behavioral and neural firing properties of monkeys. It is often referred to as *"a* biologically plausible neural network.") Across all three cases they found that learning was optimized with training occurring at 85% accuracy, 15% error. They further concluded that training at the optimal accuracy (85%) proceeds exponentially faster than training at a fixed difficulty level.

PERSISTENCE AND GRIT

Closely connected the notion of desirable difficulty and the benefits of making mistakes is the idea that progressing from novice to expert demands a level of persistence and grit. Subotnik and Jarvin (2005) argued, "Persistence through good and bad times assisted by positive reinforcement and parental pressure, prepares a developing person for the inevitable rejections or failures that are part of the growth process in talent development" (p. 347). Grit specifically refers to one's passion and perseverance for long-term goals, even in the face of difficulty. In groundbreaking research, Dr. Angela Duckworth of the University of Pennsylvania and her team discovered grit was highly corelated with conscientiousness (i.e. responsible, hard-working, organized, reliable) and accounted for significant percentage of the variance in the achievement of difficult goals (Duckworth et al., 2007).

Application of This Chapter

Recall that an organization's chief interest—and our chief interest as well—is in developing the expertise of the learners we support. Irrespective of the organization to which we

belong or the subject matter of interest, the science of expertise development stemming from psychology is highly relevant for us. Stated simply, we want to help others progress to be more expert. In practice, you might hear the term "*time-to-proficiency.*" Time-to-proficiency simply refers to the time required to get an individual proficient in the skill they were learning—the time required to get them out of the novice phase and comfortably into competence. At Facebook we used time-to-proficiency as one of three performance markers that we measured for the learners we supported.

We can then further extend the concepts of this chapter by consider a series of points regarding the four features of expertise development.

1 **Access to the mental models of expert (or "top") performers:**

- Ensure that the learning experience we design relies on the mental representations of the expert/top performers, and not lesser mental representations of mediocre performers.
- Seek those who have done an elite job themselves, or even scholars who have researched top performance. Avoid the pitfall of settling for convenience, like LinkedIn trends.
- Procure books and/or articles that are grounded in science, research, and top performance. Similarly, procure podcasts or videos that provide information from expert/top performers.

2 **Access to strong feedback:**

- Strong feedback consists of an immediate and clear articulation of the (1) desired state, (2) current state, and (3) the path for how to get from current to desired. Ensure that the learner is receiving strong, timely feedback.
- Consider this question: *"What am I doing to make possible their access to strong, timely feedback?"*

3 **Purposeful, deliberate practice:**

- First, identify the KSA that you seek to develop. Then break down the KSA into its most fundamental, basic parts. Then practice one part until mastery is achieved before moving onto the next.
- Once a learner has mastered a part, consider this question: *"What am I doing to help them incorporate multiple smaller parts of the KSA together in their actual work?"*

4 **A desirable level of difficulty as a part of their learning and practice:**

- Seek to challenge the learner such that they leave their comfort zone. Consider targeting an 85/15 ratio (or at least close to it) of successes to mistakes.
- Encourage an environment that embraces mistakes by the learner. If that is difficult, then consider revising the experience so that mistakes are less costly.

References

Baker, J., Schorer, J., Lemez, S., & Wattie, N. (2019). Understanding high achievement: The case for eminence. *Frontiers in Psychology*, 10, 1927.

Bjork, E. L., & Bjork, R. A. (2011). Making things hard on yourself, but in a good way: Creating desirable difficulties to enhance learning. In R. W. Pew, L. M. Hough, & J. R. Pomerantz (Eds.),

Psychology and the real world: Essays illustrating fundamental contributions to society (pp. 59–68). Worth.

Bjork, R. A., & Bjork, E. L. (2020). Desirable difficulties in theory and practice. *Journal of Applied Research in Memory and Cognition*, 9(4), 475.

Bonneville-Roussy, A., & Vallerand, R. J. (2020). Passion at the heart of musicians' well-being. *Psychology of Music*, 48(2), 266–282.

Chatham, R. E. (2009). The 20th century revolution in military training. In K. A. Ericsson (Ed.), *Development of professional expertise. Toward measurement of expert performance and design of optimal learning environments* (pp. 27–60). Cambridge University Press.

Chi, M. T. (2006). Two approaches to the study of experts' characteristics. In K. A. Ericsson et al. (Eds.), *The Cambridge handbook of expertise and expert performance* (pp. 21–30). Cambridge University Press.

Choudhry, N. K., Fletcher, R. H., & Soumerai, S. B. (2005). Systematic review: The relationship between clinical experience and quality of health care. *Annals of Internal Medicine*, 142(4), 260–273.

Csikszentmihalyi, M., Montijo, M. N., & Mouton, A. R. (2018). Flow theory: Optimizing elite performance in the creative realm. In S. I. Pfeiffer, E. Shaunessy-Dedrick, & M. Foley-Nicpon (Eds.), *APA handbook of giftedness and talent* (pp. 215–229). American Psychological Association. doi:10.1037/0000038-014

Danielmeier, C., & Ullsperger, M. (2011). Post-error adjustments. *Frontiers in Psychology*, 2, 233.

Dong, J., Duan, R., & Liang, S. (2022). Users' mental models of cross-device search under controlled and autonomous motivations. *Journal of Information Management*, 75(1), 68–89.

Duckworth, A. L., Peterson, C., Matthews, M. D., & Kelly, D. R. (2007). Grit: Perseverance and passion for long-term goals. *Journal of Personality and Social Psychology*, 92(6), 1087.

De Groot, A. D. (2014). *Thought and choice in chess* (vol. 4). Walter de Gruyter & Co.

Elvira, Q., Imants, J., Dankbaar, B., & Segers, M. (2017). Designing education for professional expertise development. *Scandinavian Journal of Educational Research*, 61(2), 187–204.

Ericsson, K. A., & Faivre, I. A. (1988). What's exceptional about exceptional abilities? In L. K. Obler & D. Fein (Eds.), *The exceptional brain: Neuropsychology of talent and special abilities* (pp. 436–473). Guilford Press.

Ericsson, A., & Pool, R. (2016). *Peak: Secrets from the new science of expertise.* Random House.

Ericsson, K. A., Prietula, M., & Cokely, E. (2007). The making of an expert. *Harvard Business Review*, July–August. https://hbr.org/2007/07/the-making-of-an-expert.

Fischbein, E., Tirosh, D., Stavy, R., & Oster, A. (1990). The autonomy of mental models. *For the Learning of Mathematics*, 10(1), 23–30.

Fogg, B. J. (2019). *Fogg behavior model.* Behav. Des. Lab., Stanford University.

Grape, C., Sandgren, M., Hansson, L. O., Ericson, M., & Theorell, T. (2002). Does singing promote well-being?: An empirical study of professional and amateur singers during a singing lesson. *Integrative Physiological & Behavioral Science*, 38, 65–74.

Hearst, E., & Knott, J. (2009). *Blindfold chess: History, psychology, techniques, champions, world records, and important games.* McFarland.

Johnson, P. E., Duran, A. S., Hassebrock, F., Moller, J., Prietula, M., Feltovich, P. J., & Swanson, D. B. (1981). Expertise and error in diagnostic reasoning. *Cognitive Science*, 5(3), 235–283.

Jones, N. A., Ross, H., Lynam, T., Perez, P., & Leitch, A. (2011). Mental models: An interdisciplinary synthesis of theory and methods. *Ecology and Society*, 16(1).

Kawabata, M. (2007). Virtuosity, the violin, the devil … what really made Paganini "demonic"? *Current Musicology*, 83, 85–108.

Kluger, A. N., & DeNisi, A. (1996). The effects of feedback interventions on performance: A historical review, a meta-analysis, and a preliminary feedback intervention theory. *Psychological Bulletin*, 119(2), 254.

Kruger, J., & Dunning, D. (1999). Unskilled and unaware of it: How difficulties in recognizing one's own incompetence lead to inflated self-assessments. *Journal of Personality and Social Psychology*, 77(6), 1121.

Lehmann, A. C., & Ericsson, K. A. (1998). The historical development of domains of expertise: Performance standards and innovations in music. In A. Steptoe (Ed.), *Genius and the mind: Studies of creativity and temperament in the historical record* (pp. 67–94). Oxford University Press.

Leigh, T. W., DeCarlo, T. E., Allbright, D., & Lollar, J. (2014). Salesperson knowledge distinctions and sales performance. *Journal of Personal Selling & Sales Management*, 34(2), 123–140.

Lesgold, A., Glaser, R., Rubinson, H., Feltovich, P., Klopfer, D., & Wang, Y. (2014). Expertise in a complex skill: Diagnosing x-ray pictures. In *The nature of expertise* (pp. 311–342). Psychology Press.

Monteiro, S. M., & Norman, G. (2013). Diagnostic reasoning: Where we've been, where we're going. *Teaching and Learning in Medicine*, 25(supl), S26–S32.

Nersessian, N. J. (2002). The cognitive basis of model-based reasoning in science. In P. Carruthers, S. Stich, & M. Siegal (Eds.), *The cognitive basis of science* (pp. 133–153). Cambridge University Press. doi:10.1017/CBO9780511613517.008

Olszewski-Kubilius, P., Subotnik, R. F., & Worrell, F. C. (2016). Aiming talent development toward creative eminence in the 21st century. *Roeper Review*, 38(3), 140–152.

Orr, J. M., & Carrasco, M. (2011). The role of the error positivity in the conscious perception of errors. *Journal of Neuroscience*, 31(16), 5891–5892.

Patel, V. L., Arocha, J. F., & Kaufman, D. R. (1994). Diagnostic reasoning and medical expertise. *Psychology of learning and motivation*, 31, 187–252.

Pusic, M., Pecaric, M., & Boutis, K. (2011). How much practice is enough? Using learning curves to assess the deliberate practice of radiograph interpretation. *Academic Medicine*, 86(6), 731–736.

Simonton, D. K. (1977). Eminence, creativity, and geographical marginality: A recursive structural equation model. *Journal of Personality and Social Psychology*, 35(11), 805.

Sternberg, R. J. (1998). Abilities are forms of developing expertise. *Educational Researcher*, 27(3), 11–20.

Sternberg, R. J., & Grigorenko, E. L. (1997). Are cognitive styles still in style? *American Psychologist*, 52(7), 700.

Subotnik, R. F., & Jarvin, L. (2005). Beyond expertise. In R. J. Sternberg & J. E. Davidson (Eds.), *Conceptions of giftedness* (pp. 343–357). Cambridge University Press.

Subotnik, R. F., Olszewski-Kubilius, P., & Worrell, F. C. (2011). Rethinking giftedness and gifted education: A proposed direction forward based on psychological science. *Psychological Science in the Public Interest*, 12(1), 3–54.

Westbrook, L. (2006). Mental models: A theoretical overview and preliminary study. *Journal of Information Science*, 32(6), 563–579.

Wilson, R. C., Shenhav, A., Straccia, M., & Cohen, J. D. (2019). The eighty five percent rule for optimal learning. *Nature Communications*, 10(1), 4646.

Wisniewski, B., Zierer, K., & Hattie, J. (2020). The power of feedback revisited: A meta-analysis of educational feedback research. *Frontiers in Psychology*, 10, 3087.

3 Neurodiversity, Culture, and Ethics

Chapter 3 is the third and final context-providing chapter of this book. Before diving into the specific dimensions of learning beginning in Chapter 4, it is important to highlight the fact that a large portion of this book predominantly considers the research and principles of learning regarding *neurotypical* cases. That is, in the remainder of this book I will present and explain the research for individuals whose neurological development and functioning are within the typical or expected range. However, with the hope of encouraging you to be a fully empathetic, conscientious professional, this chapter invites you to consider learners with differing abilities and neurological differences which fall under the broad classification, *neurodiverse*. Neurodiversity advocates for recognizing and accepting these variations as part of the normal spectrum of human diversity, thus promoting inclusivity and understanding across different neurotypes. It is important to note that these terms are descriptive rather than prescriptive, and they are used to engender a more inclusive and respectful understanding of neurological differences. In this chapter I will also discuss age differences, cultural differences, and ethics as well. All throughout, the focus will be on how to approach learning, with the ultimate hope being that as a professional you thoughtfully consider the various learning types, backgrounds, and perspectives of the learners you serve.

Neurodiversity

The term *neurotypical* refers to individuals who experience typical neurodevelopment and mental functioning (Jurgens, 2020). The term *neurodiverse* refers to the idea that neurological differences are natural variations of the human brain, rather than deviations or disorders. This term encompasses individuals who have neurodevelopmental conditions such as autism, ADHD, dyslexia, Tourette's syndrome, and others. In terms of prevalence, approximately 15–20% of the global population are represented as neurodiverse (Doyle, 2020). Neurodiverse individuals may have unique cognitive strengths, challenges, and ways of processing information. The neurodiversity paradigm views these differences as part of the natural spectrum of human diversity, challenging the notion that certain neurological conditions are inherently abnormal. Instead, I prefer to view them as *differences*.

To be explicitly clear, when designing instructional materials, learning experiences, and/or full developmental programs, it is essential for professionals to consider the principles of neurodiversity to thereby create inclusive and effective learning environments that account for such differences. Additionally, "accessibility," which refers to the notion that an individual can access digital content and information regardless of ability or disability, is also the goal for professionals. Let us now look at several specific differences.

DOI: 10.4324/9781003593607-4

Autism

Autism, referred to officially as autism spectrum disorder (ASD), is a neurodevelopmental difference characterized by atypical social, communicative, and motor behaviors (Dawson et al., 2008; Nemeth et al., 2010). This includes the presence of restricted and repetitive behaviors as well (Webb et al., 2017). Autism effects approximately 6 in 1,000 people. The impact of autism on learning can vary widely from person to person, as autism is a spectrum difference. While there is comparatively more research literature on the childhood and adolescent autism, here below I list several ways in which autism can affect adult learning (borrowed from Webb et al., 2017; Nemeth et al., 2010; and Dawson et al., 2008).

- **Social communication difficulties:** Individuals with autism often struggle with social interactions, which can impact communication with peers and facilitators/presenters. Challenges may include difficulty understanding and using nonverbal cues, maintaining eye contact, and engaging in reciprocal conversations. Expressive and receptive language difficulties may be present in individuals with autism. This can impact the ability to understand verbal instructions, express thoughts and ideas, and engage in effective communication.
- **Repetitive behaviors and interests:** Repetitive behaviors, such as hand-flapping or repeating certain phrases, and intense interests in specific topics can be a source of distraction which may interfere with a learner's ability to focus on academic tasks.
- **Sensory sensitivities:** Many individuals with autism experience sensory sensitivities, such as hypersensitivity to noise, lights, or textures. These sensitivities can be distracting and/or overwhelming, making it a challenge to concentrate in a typical classroom environment.
- **Difficulty with transitions:** Changes in routines or transitions between activities can be challenging for individuals with autism. This difficulty can impact the flow of the learning experience and may require additional support and planning.
- **Executive functioning challenges:** Executive functions, including skills like organization, planning, and time management, can be areas of difficulty for individuals with autism. These challenges can affect the ability to initiate and complete tasks independently.
- **Specialized learning preferences:** Some individuals with autism may have unique learning preferences and strengths. Tailoring teaching methods to accommodate these preferences can enhance the learning experience.
- **Social isolation:** Social difficulties can lead to social isolation. A lack of social engagement may impact the overall social and emotional well-being of individuals with autism.

Despite these challenges, many individuals with autism have unique talents and strengths. With appropriate support and accommodations, they can succeed in various learning environments. I provide below several strategies to consider which support learning for individuals with autism (borrowed from Webb et al., 2017; Nemeth et al., 2010; and Dawson et al., 2008).

- **Structured and visual supports:** Clear routines, visual schedules, and visual aids can provide predictability and support understanding.
- **Facial recognition:** If a learning experience includes the use of a facilitator or a talking-head style instructional video, consider only using a person/face with which an autistic learner is familiar. Such familiarity will help remove distraction in the

immediate learning experience, but also the increase the level of comfort with other social learning aspects of the overall experience.
- **Individualized instruction:** Tailor teaching methods to accommodate different learning preferences; providing individualized attention can only enhance the learning experience for learners with autism.
- **Sensory accommodations:** Provide a sensory-friendly environment and considering individual sensory preferences can create a more comfortable learning space.
- **Collaboration with learning professionals:** Working collaboratively with professionals, speech therapists, and other support personnel can contribute to a more inclusive and supportive learning environment.

Early intervention and a strengths-based approach are essential in supporting individuals with autism in their learning journey. Understanding and embracing the unique qualities of each individual can contribute to a more inclusive and positive learning experience.

Attention-Deficit/Hyperactivity Disorder

Attention-deficit/hyperactivity disorder (ADHD) is a neurodevelopmental difference that can significantly impact various aspects of learning. The core symptoms of ADHD include inattention, hyperactivity, and impulsivity. Here below I outline how ADHD can affect learning.

- **Difficulty sustaining attention:** Individuals with ADHD may struggle to maintain focus on tasks, leading to difficulties in following instructions, completing assignments, and staying engaged during lessons.
- **Impulsivity:** Impulsivity can result in hasty decision-making and actions without considering the consequences. This can affect the ability to think through problems, plan, and organize tasks effectively.
- **Hyperactivity:** While not everyone with ADHD is hyperactive, for those who are, excessive movement and restlessness can interfere with the ability to sit still and concentrate in a traditional classroom setting.
- **Executive functioning challenges:** ADHD often involves difficulties in executive functions, such as working memory, cognitive flexibility, and inhibitory control. These functions are crucial for tasks like planning, organizing, initiating and completing tasks, and managing time.
- **Procrastination and time management difficulties:** Individuals with ADHD may struggle with time perception, making it challenging to estimate how long tasks will take. This can lead to procrastination and difficulties in meeting deadlines.
- **Impaired organizational skills:** Difficulty in organizing tasks and materials can impact a learner's ability to keep track of assignments, follow schedules, and maintain a tidy workspace.
- **Social and emotional impact:** ADHD can affect social interactions and emotional regulation. Challenges in social skills and emotional control can influence relationships with peers and educators, potentially impacting the overall learning environment.
- **Underachievement:** Due to the challenges associated with ADHD, individuals may not perform up to their potential academically. This can lead to feelings of frustration, low self-esteem, and a negative impact on their overall learning experience.

However, similar to autism, it is equally crucial to realize that individuals with ADHD often have unique strengths and talents. With appropriate support and accommodations,

they can thrive with regards to learning. Strategies to support learning in individuals with ADHD may include:

- **Structured and organized learning environment:** Clear routines, visual schedules, and organized materials can help individuals with ADHD manage their tasks more effectively.
- **Breaks and movement breaks:** Providing opportunities for short breaks and incorporating movement into the learning environment can help individuals with ADHD manage restlessness.
- **Individualized instruction:** Tailoring teaching methods to accommodate different learning preferences and providing individualized attention can enhance the learning experience for learners with ADHD.
- **Use of technology and assistive tools:** Technology can be leveraged to support organization, time management, and task completion.

Dyslexia

Dyslexia is a neurological condition that affects an individual's ability to read, write, and spell. Dyslexic individuals experience a rearranged order of printed/written words. It is a specific learning difference that is often characterized by difficulties with accurate and/or fluent word recognition and by poor spelling and decoding abilities. Dyslexia is not related to intelligence; individuals with dyslexia often have average to above-average intelligence. Additionally, here below are several ways dyslexia can impact learning:

- **Reading:** Dyslexia often manifests as challenges in decoding words, recognizing sight words, and understanding the relationship between sounds and letters. This can lead to slower and less accurate reading.
- **Spelling:** Individuals with dyslexia may struggle with spelling due to difficulties in recognizing and remembering the sequence of letters in words.
- **Writing:** Expressing thoughts in writing may be challenging for individuals with dyslexia, as they may face difficulties in organizing ideas and putting them on paper.
- **Phonological processing:** Dyslexia often involves difficulties in phonological processing, which is the ability to recognize and manipulate the sounds of spoken language. This can affect the ability to break words into individual sounds and blend them together.
- **Working memory:** Dyslexia may impact working memory, making it difficult for individuals to hold and manipulate information in their minds while performing cognitive tasks, such as reading or solving problems.
- **Difficulty with sequencing:** Dyslexia can affect the ability to understand and follow sequences, such as the order of letters in words, the steps in a mathematical problem, or the sequence of events in a story.
- **Time-consuming tasks:** Reading and related tasks may take longer for individuals with dyslexia, leading to fatigue and frustration.

It is important to note that dyslexia is a spectrum disorder, and thus its impact can vary from person to person. With appropriate support, interventions, and accommodations, individuals with dyslexia can develop effective strategies to overcome many of these challenges and succeed in academic and professional settings. I list here below several research-supported strategies to enhance the learning experience for dyslexic learners (borrowed from the study conducted by MacCullagh et al., 2017).

- **Tailored support:** research suggests that traditional support services are seldom used. Therefore, instead of relying on the traditional avenues, consider a more tailored approach.
- **Adaptive note-taking techniques:** dyslexic learners that excel often used deep learning strategies, more study aids, and more coping strategies than those who get discouraged.
- **Multi-modal, multi-sensory delivery format:** videos were preferred much more over reading and listening, likely because of the audio-visual nature combined with the control of pace. At the same time, consider minimizing any auditory and visual distractions.
- **Print-on-demand course readers:** reading text online was found to be the least desirable method of consuming material for both dyslexic and non-dyslexic learners.
- **New assessment modalities:** more frequent, shorter, lower-weighted assessment tasks were preferred by adult learners.

Tourette's Syndrome

Tourette's syndrome is a neurological difference characterized by involuntary, repetitive movements and sounds known as *tics.* Motor tics can consist of eye blinking, grimaces, touching, and banging. Evidence suggests that such involuntary motor movement is the result of "structural and functional abnormalities of the basal ganglia" (Kéri et al., 2002, p. 1356). Vocal tics can consist of throat clearing, snorting, growling, or words and phrases that occasionally carry obscene or aggressive themes. Taken together, the motor and vocal tics associated with Tourette's often begin in childhood and can range from mild to severe. While there is no evidence to suggest Tourette's itself does not directly affect cognitive abilities, research does suggest that it can impact learning in several ways that I outline here below (this list is largely taken from Kéri et al., 2002).

- **Distraction:** Tics, both motor and vocal, can be distracting for the individual with Tourette's and for others in a training room. This distraction can interfere with concentration and focus on learning tasks.
- **Emotional impact**: Dealing with a chronic condition like Tourette's can contribute to stress and anxiety, which can, in turn, affect a learner's overall well-being and ability to engage with academic tasks.
- **Social challenges:** Individuals with Tourette's may experience social challenges due to their tics. This can lead to feelings of isolation and/or bullying, which can impact their emotional well-being and, consequently, their ability to engage in learning activities.
- **Attention difficulties:** Some individuals with Tourette's may also experience attention difficulties, similar to ADHD. These attention challenges can affect the ability to sustain focus on learning tasks.
- **Impact on organization and time management:** Tics can disrupt the flow of tasks and may require additional time for completion. This can affect a learner's ability to manage time efficiently and meet deadlines.
- **The stigma:** Misunderstandings about Tourette's can lead to stigma and biases in learning settings. Professionals may not always be aware of the nature of the disorder, leading to misconceptions and potentially hindering the learning environment.

Despite these challenges, many individuals with Tourette's can excel academically with appropriate support and accommodations. Strategies to support learning in individuals with Tourette's may include:

- **Providing a supportive and understanding learning environment:** Professionals who are aware of Tourette's and its characteristics can create a more inclusive and supportive atmosphere.
- **Accommodations for tics:** Flexible arrangements, such as allowing breaks when needed or providing alternative ways to demonstrate understanding, can be helpful.
- **Collaboration with support professionals:** Working with support professionals or physicians can help develop strategies to address specific challenges and promote academic success.

It's essential to recognize the individual nature of Tourette's and tailor support to the specific needs of each learner. Early intervention and a collaborative approach involving educators, parents, and healthcare professionals can contribute to a positive learning experience for individuals with Tourette's syndrome.

Key Principles

In sum, when working with neurodiverse individuals, failure to consider abilities of all types may result in individuals experiencing obstacles to their learning, limiting the effectiveness of the learning experience for them. Additionally, those designing the learning experience and/or the learners themselves will likely incur additional costs in time and resources to make adjustments and accommodations. Instead, please consider the following key principles.

Diverse Learning Preferences

- Understand and acknowledge that learners have diverse neurological profiles, and there is no one-size-fits-all approach to learning. (Please consider this the Golden Rule: there is no one-size-fits all.)
- Design instructional materials that cater to different learning preferences, incorporating visual, auditory, kinesthetic, and other modalities. (Remember, these are simply learning preferences, not styles.)

Flexibility and Customization

- Recognize that neurodiverse learners may benefit from personalized and flexible learning paths. Provide options for learners to choose activities or assessments that align with their strengths and preferences.
- Allow for variations in the pace of learning, as some neurodiverse individuals may need more time to process information or complete tasks.

Clear Communication

- Present information in a clear, concise, and consistent manner. Avoid ambiguity and provide explicit instructions to support neurodiverse learners who may benefit from clarity.
- Use visual aids, diagrams, and other visual supports to enhance understanding. Visual information can be particularly helpful for neurodiverse individuals who may process information better through visual channels.

Sensory Considerations

- Be mindful of sensory sensitivities. Design learning materials and spaces to be sensory-friendly, considering factors such as lighting, noise levels, and the use of sensory-friendly tools or accommodations.

Inclusive Assessment

- Implement a variety of assessment methods that accommodate different strengths and challenges. Consider alternatives to traditional written assessments, such as project-based assessments or oral presentations.
- Provide flexibility in assessment timing to accommodate neurodiverse learners who may need additional time or breaks.

Supportive Environment

- Foster an inclusive and supportive classroom culture. Encourage understanding and acceptance of neurodiversity among learners and facilitators/presenters.
- Facilitate peer support and collaboration. Encourage neurotypical learners to work with neurodiverse peers, promoting a sense of community and mutual learning.

Technology Integration

- Ensure that instructional materials and learning platforms are accessible to neurodiverse learners. Consider the use of assistive technologies that can support different needs, such as text-to-speech tools or screen readers.

Continuous Professional Development

- Provide ongoing training for educators on neurodiversity and inclusive teaching practices. Equip instructional designers and facilitators/presenters with the knowledge and skills needed to create neurodiverse-friendly learning environments.

Respect for Neurodiverse Perspectives

- Use respectful and inclusive language when discussing neurodiversity. Avoid stigmatizing language and stereotypes, promoting a positive and accepting attitude towards neurodiverse individuals.

Collaboration with Stakeholders

- Collaborate with neurodiverse individuals, caregivers, and advocacy groups to gather insights and feedback. Involving diverse perspectives ensures that learning design efforts are more responsive to the needs of neurodiverse learners.

By incorporating these principles of neurodiversity into instructional design, educators and instructional designers can create learning environments that celebrate differences, support individual strengths, and provide opportunities for all learners to succeed.

Age Considerations

Keeping with the spirit of this chapter, it is important to also discuss the considerations related to age. The statistics are clear: many adults experience a loss of hearing, sight, and/or memory as they age. Any loss in hearing or sight will invariably impact sensory memory. Research has shown that memory impairment resulting from age is due to a variety of neurodegenerative factors, including: neural necrosis (i.e. neural cell death), apoptosis (i.e. natural, programmed cell death), excitotoxicity (i.e. glutamate's mediation of the death of central neurons), oxidative stress (i.e. when the amount of oxidizing agents is greater than antioxidant capacity), mitochondria dysfunction (i.e. a malfunction with the brain's energy metabolism), and autophagic dysfunction (i.e. autophagia is the process of removing damaged cellular components—so a decrease in or impairment of autophagic events has shown to contribute to Alzheimer's) (Toricelli et al., 2021).

While most remedies for the effect of age on memory are pharmacological in nature, there are two that are not. Toricelli et al. (2021) stated, "Both physical activity and environmental enrichment have been seen as a means of improving memory and learning as well as increasing hippocampal neurogenesis" (p. 7). However, I will discuss the principles of improving memory and learning in further detail in Chapters 4 and 5.

Culture

Culture plays a significant and multifaceted role in the learning process, influencing instructional methods, communication styles, and the overall learning environment, whether it is in-person or remote. I present here below several ways in which culture impacts the learning process.

- **Personal identity:** Learners bring their cultural backgrounds and identities into the learning environment. Understanding and respecting learners' diverse cultural identities contribute to a more inclusive and supportive atmosphere.
- **Self-concept:** Cultural context shapes how individuals perceive themselves and their roles in society. The learning process should acknowledge and affirm learners' self-concept within their cultural framework.
- **Teaching and learning preferences:** Different cultures may have distinct preferences for learning. Some cultures may emphasize collaborative learning, while others may value independent study. Professionals need to be aware of and incorporate diverse teaching methods to accommodate various learning preferences.
- **Language development:** Language is a significant aspect of culture. Recognizing and valuing linguistic diversity in the classroom is crucial for effective communication and learning. Professionals should consider language differences and provide support for any learners learning in a second language.
- **Cultural relevance in curriculum:** A culturally responsive curriculum reflects the diversity of learners' backgrounds and experiences. Including a variety of perspectives, authors, historical events, and cultural contexts in the curriculum enhances the relevance of the material and engages learners more effectively.
- **Social interaction and communication:** Cultural differences can influence communication styles, including non-verbal communication, norms of politeness, and approaches to conflict resolution. Facilitators/presenters and learners may have diverse expectations regarding communication, and understanding these differences is essential for effective interaction.
- **Values and beliefs:** Culture shapes individuals' values and ethical beliefs. The learning process provides an opportunity to explore and discuss diverse ethical perspectives, fostering a deeper understanding of different value systems.

- **Global perspectives and citizenship:** Learning should equip learning with cultural competence, helping them understand and navigate diverse cultural landscapes. This is increasingly important in a globalized world where cross-cultural communication and collaboration are common.
- **Cultural celebrations and traditions:** Recognizing and celebrating cultural holidays, traditions, and events in the learning environment fosters a sense of belonging and respect. It also helps break down stereotypes and promotes a positive appreciation for diversity.
- **Cultural sensitivity and equity:** Cultural sensitivity is crucial for promoting equity in learning. Being aware of and addressing cultural biases and stereotypes helps create a fair and inclusive learning environment for all learners.

In essence, recognizing and incorporating cultural elements into the learning design process enriches the learning experience, fosters inclusivity, and prepares learners to navigate a diverse and interconnected professional world. L&D professionals and organizations play a key role in creating culturally responsive learning environments that honor and leverage the cultural assets of their learners.

Ethics

Ethics play a crucial role in the learning process, influencing the behavior of learners, L&D professionals, and the overall learning environment. Here below I present several key aspects of the role of ethics in the learning process.

- **Respect for others:** Ethics in learning environments demands an emphasis on the treating others with respect, regardless of differences in background, beliefs, or abilities. This fosters a positive and inclusive learning environment.
- **Integrity:** Professionals and learners are expected to uphold high ethical standards, promoting honesty, and discouraging cheating or plagiarism. Upholding integrity is vital for the credibility of the learning process.

Social Responsibility

- **Community engagement:** Ethical learning encourages a sense of social responsibility. Learners are often encouraged to engage with their communities, promoting social justice and contributing positively to society.
- **Global citizenship:** Learning about global issues and promoting ethical behavior on a global scale are often parts of learning within organization settings. This helps learners develop a sense of responsibility for the well-being of the broader community.

Critical Thinking and Decision-Making

- **Ethical reasoning:** Learning experiences should facilitate the development of ethical reasoning skills. Learners should be encouraged to think critically about moral issues, consider diverse perspectives, and make informed, ethically sound decisions.
- **Problem-solving:** Ethical principles provide a framework for addressing complex problems. In the learning process, learners can apply ethical reasoning to real-world situations, enhancing their problem-solving skills.

Inclusivity and Diversity

- **Promoting diversity:** Ethical with respect the learning emphasizes the importance of valuing and celebrating diversity. This includes recognizing and respecting different cultures, perspectives, and backgrounds, creating an inclusive learning environment.
- **Equity:** Ethical considerations with respect to learning involves promoting equity and ensuring that all learners have access to a quality learning experience, regardless of socio-economic status, race, gender, or other factors.

Professional Conduct

- **Modeled ethics:** Facilitators and presenters play a significant role in modeling ethical behavior. They are expected to adhere to professional codes of conduct, demonstrating integrity, fairness, and a commitment to the well-being of their learners.
- **Learner behavior:** Learners are expected to adhere to ethical standards as well. This includes treating peers and facilitators/presenters respectfully, completing tasks honestly, and participating in the learning process with integrity.
- **Technology and information ethics:** In an era of increasing technology use, ethical considerations extend to how information is accessed, used, and shared. Learners need to develop digital citizenship skills (e.g. being a strong teammate in an online course, wink wink), understanding the ethical implications of online behavior and information consumption.

In summary, ethics in the learning process promotes a positive, inclusive, and responsible learning environment. It helps learners develop not only academic knowledge but also the moral and ethical foundations that contribute to their overall character and societal contributions.

References

Dawson, M., Mottron, L., & Gernsbacher, M. A. (2008). Learning in autism. *Learning and Memory*, 2, 759–772.

Doyle, N. (2020). Neurodiversity at work: A biopsychosocial model and the impact on working adults. *British Medical Bulletin*, 135(1), 108.

Evans, D., Granson, M., Langford, D., & Hirsch, S. (2023). Autism spectrum disorder: Reconceptualizing support for neurodiverse students in higher education. *Journal of Higher Education Policy and Management*, 45(2), 243–257. doi:10.1080/1360080X.2023.2180168.

Hamilton, L. G., & Petty, S. (2023). Compassionate pedagogy for neurodiversity in higher education: A conceptual analysis. *Frontiers in Psychology*, 14, 1093290.

Hand, C. J. (2023). Neurodiverse undergraduate psychology students' experiences of presentations in education and employment. *Journal of Applied Research in Higher Education*, 15(5), 1600–1617.

Jurgens, A. (2020). Neurodiversity in a neurotypical world. In H. Rosqvist, N. Chown, & A. Stenning (Eds.), *Neurodiversity studies: A new critical paradigm* (pp. 73–88). Routledge.

Kéri, S., Szlobodnyik, C., Benedek, G., Janka, Z., & Gádoros, J. (2002). Probabilistic classification learning in Tourette syndrome. *Neuropsychologia*, 40(8), 1356–1362.

MacCullagh, L., Bosanquet, A., & Badcock, N. A. (2017). University students with dyslexia: A qualitative exploratory study of learning practices, challenges and strategies. *Dyslexia*, 23(1), 3–23.

Nemeth, D., Janacsek, K., Balogh, V., Londe, Z., Mingesz, R., Fazekas, M., … & Vetro, A. (2010). Learning in autism: Implicitly superb. *PloS one*, 5(7), e11731.

Shmulsky, S., Gobbo, K., & Vitt, S. (2022). Culturally relevant pedagogy for neurodiversity. *Community College Journal of Research and Practice*, 46(9), 681–685, doi:10.1080/10668926.2021.1972362.

Toricelli, M., Pereira, A. A. R., Abrao, G. S., Malerba, H. N., Maia, J., Buck, H. S., & Viel, T. A. (2021). Mechanisms of neuroplasticity and brain degeneration: Strategies for protection during the aging process. *Neural Regeneration Research*, 16(1), 58.

Webb, S. J., Neuhaus, E., & Faja, S. (2017). Face perception and learning in autism spectrum disorders. *Quarterly Journal of Experimental Psychology*, 70(5), 970–986.

Part II

The Cognitive Dimension of Learning

4 The Central Nervous System and Memory

The Case of Patient H.M.

Medical patient Henry Molaison, known in the annals of medicine as "Patient H.M.," is likely the most famous patient in all of neuroscience (Squire, 2009). In an accident in 1930 at the age of seven, H.M. was hit hard and knocked down by a bicycle. Three years later at age 10 he began to experience minor seizures, which then progressed to major epileptic seizures by age 16. By 1953, H.M. was so incapacitated by his seizures that he struggled to work or live a normal life. He consulted with neurosurgeon Dr. William Scoville, who offered H.M. an experimental procedure that he carried out before with several of his other patients. The procedure would involve removing H.M.'s hippocampus—the part of the brain believed to be the source of his seizures at the time. After consulting with his family, H.M. agreed and the surgery was then performed later in 1953.

Back in 1953, however, neither H.M.'s neurosurgeon nor the rest of the medical community were fully aware of the true function of the hippocampus and its specific role in memory. On one hand, the surgery was a success, as H.M. did in fact experience fewer seizures. However, his family noticed soon after the procedure that H.M. started suffering from amnesia, which persisted well past the time he was expected to fully recover. He now lacked the ability to form new memories, causing him to perpetually live an existence of moment-to-moment forgetfulness for decades to come. He described his new state in this way: "like waking from a dream … every day is alone in itself" (Squire et al., 2009, p. 1). Therein began the scientific world's fascination with H.M., and the relationship between the hippocampus and human memory. Over the next few decades, H.M. would be the focus of many research studies that would bring about the discovery of much knowledge to the world.

Overview

Why is H.M. the most famous neuroscience patient in history? In our exploration of adult learning, why is understanding the brain so critical? The answer is simple: the brain gives rise to the mind, and our mind is responsible for all mental and cognitive functioning. For example, the brain is the processing center for perception. We perceive the world around us through our brain's constant processing of what we see (vision), hear (audio), and feel/touch (motor sensory inputs). In this book, however, our primary concern is the mental function of cognition—that is, how we think about the people, things, and world around us. I begin with a historic look at the way scientists have studied human cognition thus far.

DOI: 10.4324/9781003593607-6

Cognitivism

Through much of history into the twentieth century, little was known about the human brain and its true capabilities. As a result, theories such as behaviorism (i.e. outwardly observable behaviors) dominated the landscape of human learning (I discuss behaviorism in depth in Chapter 8). Then approximately 60–70 years ago, a flurry of important academic papers was published by American psychologists dissatisfied by behaviorism's dominance of the field, and its relaxed attitude towards studying human consciousness. This cognitive revolution signified a seismic shift towards trying to see inside the *black box* of our minds to better explain how humans process, recall, and retain information. Scholars such as Jerome Bruner (who studied sensation and visual perception), both Jean Piaget and Lev Vygotsky (the psychological development of children), Ulric Neisser (cognitive psychology), and Benjamin Bloom (Bloom's Taxonomy) each contributed to the early development of cognitivism. The theory of cognitivism includes the following tenets:

- Learning is a mental process of organizing information into conceptualized models of related ideas and concepts, also known as schemas.
- Knowledge is actively constructed in the mind and mediated by experience.
- Instruction needs to be organized, sequenced, and presented in a manner that is understandable and meaningful to the learner's psyche.
- Memory plays a central role in how a person interprets and understands the world around them.

For so long, little was known definitively about how the brain processes information, which allowed the theory of cognitivism to become the central dogma in psychology for much of the twentieth century. However, through advances in neuroscience, imaging, and research on individuals just like H.M., we now understand so much more scientifically about the underlying neural circuitry of the human brain involved in learning than we did decades ago. Thus, the advances and findings of neuroscience research have replaced the void that cognitivism once filled; that is, the explanatory power of the cognitivism is reduced. As such, the remainder of this chapter and the following chapter will focus on these important discoveries and how neuroscience relates to human learning and performance.

The Central Nervous System

Understanding the central nervous system (CNS) helps us grasp the mechanisms involved in memory and learning. As practitioners, the more we know and understand the mechanisms of memory and learning, the more effective we can—and should—be. Therefore, while this chapter largely covers the *anatomy* of the CNS, Chapter 5 will shift focus to the *physiology* of how the different parts of the CNS contribute to learning. The CNS is the processing center of the human body and is made of the brain and spinal cord. It is a complex system that processes the inputs we receive from and experiences we have with the outside world, and then coordinates our sensations, perceptions, and actions in response. Our bodies simply would not be able to operate without the CNS.

The Neuron

We begin with the neuron, which is the fundamental cell of the CNS. Neurons are composed of three parts: the cell body, a long axon, and a short dendrite. The human brain contains approximately 85–90 billion neurons. The *cell body* of the neuron contains the

nucleus which is similar to the nucleus of every other cell in our body in that it controls the cell's activities and contains the cell's genetic material (i.e. DNA). The *axon* resembles a tail and sends messages from the neuron. To assist in the sending of messages, axons are covered by a layer of fat known as the *myelin sheath*, which serves to help conduct neural signals faster. The *dendrites* resemble tree branches and receive inputs/messages from other cells.

Neurons communicate with one another via the synapse. A *synapse* is a small gap between two neurons, where nerve impulses are relayed by a chemical neurotransmitter from the axon of a presynaptic (sending) neuron to the dendrite of a postsynaptic (receiving) neuron. Think of a synapse as a connection point between two neurons. Regardless of neuron type, there are six to ten thousand total synapses on each neuron (Dehaene, 2021). As we extrapolate that across our entire brain, this equates to over 100 trillion total synapses, or neural connection points, in our brains.

There are three types of neurons in the human brain: sensory neurons, motor neurons, and interneurons.

1 **Sensory neurons.** Sensory neurons are the nerve cells that are activated by sensory input (e.g. sound, touch, heat, or light) from the environment. For example, when you touch something hot, the sensory neurons are those which fire and send signals to the rest of the nervous system about the information they have received. The inputs that activate sensory neurons can be physical or chemical, corresponding to all five of our senses. A chemical input comes from taste or smell, which neurons then send to the brain. Whereas a physical input includes feelings of touch and pressure, or when certain wavelengths of light are perceived as various colors. Most sensory neurons are pseudounipolar, which means they only have one axon which extends slightly from the cell body before splitting into two branches.
2 **Motor neurons.** Motor neurons connect the muscles, glands, and organs throughout the body. They do this by sending impulses from the spinal cord to the skeletal and

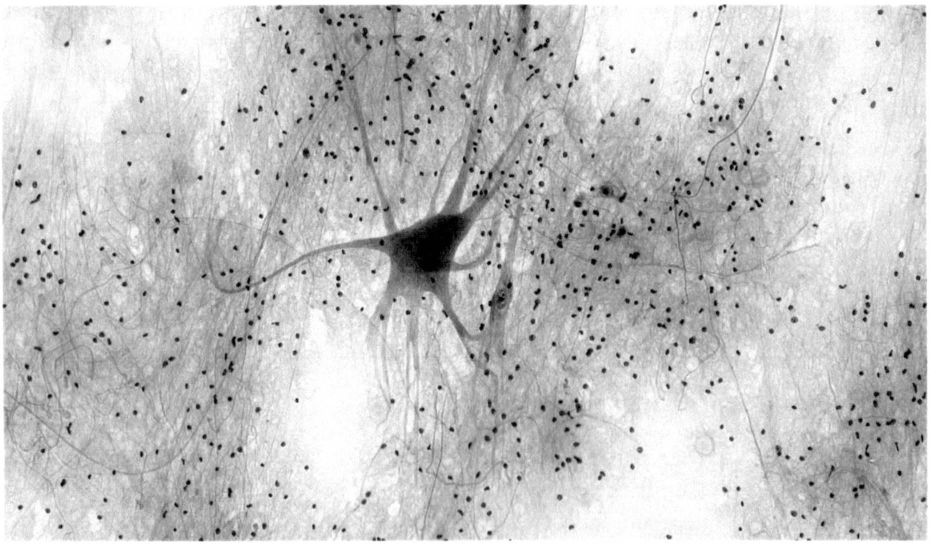

Figure 4.1 Structure of a neuron

smooth muscles (such as those in your stomach). Therefore, motor neurons are responsible for directly controlling all voluntary and involuntary muscle movements. Motor neurons are divided into two subcategories: those that travel from spinal cord to muscle are called *lower motor neurons*; and those that travel between the brain and spinal cord are called *upper motor neurons*. Motor neurons have the most common type shape for a nerve cell: they are multipolar, each with one axon and several dendrites.

3 **Interneurons.** Interneurons connect sensory and spinal motor neurons. Their main role is to transfer signals between the two. However, interneurons also communicate with each other, forming circuits of various complexity. They are multipolar, just like motor neurons.

Major Components of the Brain

There are four major components of the brain: (1) the cerebral cortex, (2) the combination of the brainstem and cerebellum, (3) the limbic system, and (4) the white matter. Obviously, there are more parts to the brain, but these comprise the major four.

Cerebral Cortex

The cerebral cortex is the outer layer that envelops the brain. The front part of the cerebral cortex is known as the prefrontal cortex, and is responsible for executive functions that include planning, goal setting, self-control, schema development, and attention and focus. Different primary sensory regions of the cerebral cortex also do different things. However, each region has a "map." There are three key ways in which different cortical areas on the map distinguish themselves: (1) by specific, distinct *function*; (2) by a distinct *connectivity* fingerprint; and (3) by distinctive *layer* (i.e. it physically looks different).

Brainstem and Cerebellum

The brainstem and cerebellum are located in the bottommost region of the brain (see the image below). The brainstem relays information from the brain to the cerebellum, then to the spinal cord. The brainstem regulates breathing, consciousness, and body temperature. And while the brainstem is not important cognitively, but it is necessary for sustaining life. That is, a person can stay alive without the cerebral cortex, but a person cannot stay alive without a brainstem.

The cerebellum is involved in motor coordination. Skill memory is processed in the cerebellum, which then relays information to the basal ganglia (discussed below). The basal ganglia stores automatic learned memories like tying a shoe, playing an instrument, or riding a bike. At present, there is debate and a lack of clarity as to the cerebellum's role in cognition.

Limbic System

The limbic system is the part of the brain involved in our behavioral and emotional responses, especially when it comes to behaviors we need for survival: feeding, reproduction, caring for our young, and fight or flight responses. The structures of the limbic system are buried deeper within the brain, underneath the cerebral cortex but above the brainstem, and consists of the *thalamus*, *hippocampus*, and *amygdala*. There are also two smaller structures involved in the actions of the limbic system, but are considered minor compared to the thalamus, hippocampus, and amygdala: (1) the hypothalamus (a subregion of the

thalamus) which is responsible for production of important hormones and regulation of thirst, hunger, mood etc.; and (2) basal ganglia, which is responsible for reward processing, habit formation, movement, and learning.

Thalamus

The thalamus is the "grand central station" of the brain, as it receives and initially processes most of the incoming sensory information (audible, visual, touch). (Note: olfaction does not go through the thalamus; instead, it goes straight to the olfactory cortex.) The neurons of the thalamus are bidirectional, running in both the incoming and outgoing directions.

Hippocampus

The hippocampus (Greek for "seahorse") resembles the shape of a seahorse and serves as the memory center of our brains. It is an intermediate storage area of information (research shows up to 4 years), before it goes into long-term memory in the cerebral cortex. Ultimately, the hippocampus helps us define ourselves as we grow and experience life. Do you recall from the beginning of the chapter that patient H.M. lost the ability to form new memories once he had his hippocampus removed? We now know that this occurred because our episodic memories are formed and initially cataloged in the hippocampus, and then sent to long-term storage across other (non-hippocampus) parts of the cerebral cortex. In short, the hippocampus helps us form *new memories* (Suzuki, 2007). So by having his hippocampus removed, while H.M. could still recall facts from his past, he essentially lost the ability to add new memories to his long-term storage, resulting in feeling like each day was new, with no recollection of the period of time immediately preceding it. To be clear, much of what is known today about the hippocampus results from research done from individuals who had their hippocampus removed—in this manner, we are indebted to H.M. and others like him.

Connections made in the hippocampus also help us associate memories with various senses. For example, the hippocampus is the part of the brain where the association between the smell of pine trees and the Christmas season would be formed. In a similar vein, the hippocampus helps us imagine or envision situations that we have never been in before while also being important for spatial recognition, orientation, and our ability to navigate the world through the recall of spatial information. Putting all of these functions together, the hippocampus helps us make associations with anything past, present, or even imagined into the future.

But one of the most important roles of the hippocampus, however, is its involvement in *neuroplasticity*, which is the key biological phenomenon in learning. Neuroplasticity refers to the brain's ability to adapt and change through the strengthening or weakening of neural connections, and the growth of new neurons altogether. The hippocampus is one of the key sites of the brain where new neurons are made from adult stem cells. The process of the growth of new neurons from stem cells is called *neurogenesis*, and is one form of neuroplasticity. We will discuss neuroplasticity in greater depth in the next chapter.

Amygdala

The amygdala (Greek for "almond") is part of the temporal lobe. It is a small, paired structure, meaning you have two of them, one on each side of your brain. However, scientists typically refer to the amygdala pair using the singular form of the word. Your amygdala sits near several structures that carry information from your senses, especially

smell, which is why scents can connect strongly to emotions and memories. Your amygdala also connects to brain areas that process vision and hearing. Vertically, your amygdala is nearly level with your eyes. If you touch your fingertip to the temple of your head (just above the joint where your jawbone connects to your skull) and point directly toward the temple on the opposite side of your head, you will be pointing at your amygdala or very near it.

As far as the function is concerned, the Amygdala is the main processor of our emotions. Fear is the key emotion that the amygdala is known to control. That is why the amygdala is so important to survival (think *fight or flight*)—because it processes things we see or hear and uses that input to learn what is dangerous. Then if you encounter something similar in the future, your amygdala will cause you to feel fear or similar emotions. Research also shows a connection between the amygdala and the ability to store emotional memories. In fact, research on people with amygdala damage shows impairment in remembering details of the emotionally charging portion of a story, despite having normal memory for the remaining elements of the story that were non-emotional (Cahill et al., 1995). However, research also shows that the amygdala contributes to more than just anxiety or fear. It also plays a role in the following:

- Aggression.
- Learning through rewards and punishment.
- Handling and using implicit (unconscious) memory, which allows you to remember how to do certain things without remembering how you learned them (like riding a bike or tying your shoes).
- Social communication and understanding, including how you interpret someone's intentions from how they talk or act.
- Emotions that relate to parenting and caregiving.
- Emotions we connect to memories.
- Learned behaviors related to addiction.

White Matter

White matter makes up 45% of the human brain and consists of the axons which connect cell bodies. White matter provides the communication between different gray matter areas. (The gray matter represents the areas where the actual "processing" is done.) This high percentage of white matter in the brain is due to all the cables that connect the remote parts of the brain. Lastly, white matter tends to be inflexible (Knowland & Thomas, 2014).

Memory

Like an orchestra whose many sections must work together to produce a symphony, memory is a complex process. The creation of long-term memory involves many stages, as well as many areas of the brain. Specifically, the process of memory includes three phases: encoding, storage, and retrieval. *Encoding* refers to how our brains experience the world around us, decide what information from that experience is important (i.e. what to focus on), and begin to move that information to storage. Deciding what to focus on takes place in the thalamus. *Storage* refers to the creation of a permanent record of information in one's long-term memory. In order for a memory to go into storage in long-term memory, it must pass through three distinct stages: sensory memory, working memory, and then finally long-term memory. The storage phase of memory takes place in the amygdala and hippocampus. *Retrieval* (or *recall*) is simply one's ability to access information that is stored

in their long-term memory. There are different areas of the brain involved in these various phases of memory. Let us now look at each one.

Sensory Memory

Before we can learn something, we must first perceive it. Before we perceive it, we must first sense it. Sensing, observing, and experiencing the world around us is how our brain initially takes in new information; perception is the process of interpreting it (Weinstein et al., 2018). We specifically take in sensory information from the world around us through what we see, hear, and feel. This sensory processing occurs in the thalamus.

Working (or Short-term) Memory

Working memory (WM), which is also referred to as short-term memory, occurs in the prefrontal cortex (PFC), which is the frontmost region of our cerebral cortex (think: the region directly behind your forehead). The PFC stores information for only a few seconds unless consistently rehearsed (Baddeley, 1992), and its capacity is limited to about 5–7 items as part of complex cognitive tasks (Miller, 1956).

Working memory is the system of memory where all conscious thinking takes place. It is in the working memory of the prefrontal cortex where active processing occurs (Clark, 2008). In fact, working memory stands at the crossroads between attention, intentionality, perception, and memory (Baddeley, 2003). (We will discuss the role of *attention* in greater depth in Chapter 5.) Working memory restricts the range of immediate and quick changes to the long-term memory (LTM) and acts as a center for conscious information processing and short term maintenance. Recall from Chapter 2 that our mental models are dynamic in nature and therefore referred to as "working models." Well, research has shown that an individual's "mental model is constructed in working memory. Working memory is the system responsible for selecting and manipulating information for the purpose of reasoning and learning" (Jones et al., 2011, p 4). We actively reconstruct knowledge and memories in our working memory, meaning that learning begins in our WM when we take in new information from different sources before comparing and integrating that data with prior knowledge structures stored in long-term memory.

For example, the working memory in the PFC enables you to remember a phone number someone just shared with you. However, our working memory can be easily overworked (or "overloaded") if more than a few chunks of information are processed at once, a phenomenon which is referred to as *cognitive overload* (Sweller, 1994). (The amount of processing required by one's working memory is generally known as the *cognitive load.*) During cognitive overload, the learner's cognitive processing exceeds the learner's available cognitive capacity. In other words, the processing demands evoked by the learning task exceed the processing capacity of the cognitive system. Cognitive overload hinders new information from integrating with prior knowledge stored in long-term memory and therefore cannot be used to construct new knowledge. To be explicitly clear, cognitive overload is very much a suboptimal condition because it impedes learning.

Working memory consists of three separate parts: a central executive system, and two subordinate systems: the *visuospatial sketch pad* and the *phonological loop*. The *central executive system* is concerned with the intentional control of behavior. The *visuospatial sketch pad* is closely related to visual perception. The *phonological loop* is closely related to speech perception and speech production. However, each of these components of WM are limited in their individual processing power where, for example, your phonological loop is

busy doing something else, it cannot help you retain information, such as reciting a poem out loud while trying to remember a phone number (Weinstein et al., 2018).

Encoding Into Long-Term Memory

Encoding is the means by which information is stored into long-term memory. Long-term memory is processed in the hippocampus of the temporal lobe and is activated when you want to remember or memorize something for a longer time. Most memory failures occur during the encoding process when attempting to store new information.

In contrast to the limits of working memory, our long-term memory has a seemingly unlimited storage capacity. Long-term memory contains two types of memories: *explicit memories*, which can be recalled consciously such as personal experiences (e.g. getting your first pet) as well as factual information (2 + 2 = 4). Conversely, *implicit memories* are those which cannot be recollected in our consciousness and include tacit knowledge as well as various forms of learned associations including concept learning (e.g. all birds have wings, beaks, and feathers) and phobias.

Memory Recall (or Retrieval)

New knowledge encoded in LTM needs to be recalled/found/“retrieved” in order to be used. If this does not happen, it becomes a transfer failure. The goal of any learning or training exercise is for learners to be able to recall (or “transfer”) information from their LTM back into WM from which to use in their work (Clark, 2008). While there are several techniques that research has shown can improve the likelihood of successful information retrieval, I will offer three of the most effective here: the use of *imagery, context*, and *repetition*.

Imagery

Imagery involves attaching a mental image to a verbal idea. Doing so forces the brain to “dually encode” information in both verbal and visual spatial memory areas. Using imagery allows the learner to combine multiple unrelated verbal ideas into a single image, which lessens the total amount of processing needed for retrieval. Images are more powerful when specific to the person, such as visualizing *your* mother or *your* favorite coffee mug. You may have heard the adage, “A picture is worth 1,000 words.” Well, a movie is worth 10,000 pictures. Any time an individual looks at things that have visual motion, their attention system will naturally gravitate toward the movement. This means that with all things being equal, motion graphics that support the learning objectives are superior to still graphics at enhancing the learning experience; similarly, still graphics are better than text-only.

Context

Similarly, the additional detail from context adds semantic meaning to a verbal idea. You can consider this akin to crafting a narrative around the information you are trying to remember. For example, if your shopping list includes a “mop” and some “hot sauce,” it will be more easily remembered if you imagine a janitor cleaning up a hot sauce spill than by remembering the two items individually. So contextualized learning, when supported with imagery, can be a powerful recipe for helping people encode information into their long-term memory. This holds true even for those who have suffered traumatic brain injuries affecting memory.

Repetition

Our brains remap information when we have to use effort to retrieve that information, thus helping to cement the information longer-term. Not surprisingly, the more we repeat the retrieval of information, the stronger the connections become. "Effortful retrieval both strengthens the memory but also makes the learning pliable again, leading to its reconsolidation. Reconsolidation helps update your memories with new information and connect them to more recent learning" (Brown et al., 2014, p. 100). Along this idea:

> Memory has some similarities to a Google search algorithm, in the sense that the more you connect what you learn to what you already know, and the more associations you make to a memory (for example, linking it with a visual image, a place, or a larger story), then the more mental cues you have through which to find and retrieve the memory again later.
>
> (Brown et al., 2014, p. 112)

To summarize: each time we retrieve information, we reorganize and reinforce our mental representations. As new knowledge is introduced, we have better representations to connect it to, and the more likely we are to remember it.

One of the differences between a Google search algorithm and human memory is that human memory is *reconstructive* (Weinstein et al., 2018). That is, every time you retrieve a memory, you have the potential to change it, so recalling information correctly strengthens your memory.

Application of This Chapter

This chapter has focused predominantly on the anatomy of the central nervous system. As such, the application will be limited. However, based on what we know about the impact of imagery, context, and repetition on memory recall, let us consider how a professional might apply this knowledge to the workplace.

Regarding *imagery*, professionals designing learning experiences can consider replacing large blocks of text with images, charts, diagrams, etc. Moreover, because motion is so captivating to the brain of the person viewing, consider implementing motion graphics and/or videos, whenever appropriate, if possible. Regarding *context*, I am a firm believer that, regardless of the subject, providing the learner with as much background detail as possible is the best option. Additionally, do you recall that one of Knowles's assumptions is the adult learner's preference to know why? Explaining the underlying reasons (i.e. the why) behind a concept is always a sound practice. Lastly regarding *repetition*, the more a learner can be exposed to a concept, the better. Therefore, for critical concepts, consider introducing learners to a concept multiple times as a thread throughout the learning experience instead of relying on a single, heavy dose.

References

Baddeley, A. (1992). Working memory. *Science*, 255(5044), 556–559.

Baddeley, A. (2003). Working memory: Looking back and looking forward. *Nature Reviews Neuroscience*, 4(10), 829–839.

Brown, P. C., RoedigerIII, H. L., & McDaniel, M. A. (2014). *Make it stick: The science of successful learning*. Harvard University Press.

Cahill, L., Babinsky, R., Markowitsch, H. J., & McGaugh, J. L. (1995). The amygdala and emotional memory. *Nature*, 377, 295–296.

Clark, R. C. (2008). *Building expertise: Cognitive methods for training and performance improvement.* John Wiley & Sons.

Dehaene, S. (2021). *How we learn: Why brains learn better than any machine … for now.* Penguin.

Jones, N. A., Ross, H., Lynam, T., Perez, P., & Leitch, A. (2011). Mental models: An interdisciplinary synthesis of theory and methods. *Ecology and Society*, 16(1), 46.

Knowland, V. C., & Thomas, M. S. (2014). Educating the adult brain: How the neuroscience of learning can inform educational policy. *International Review of Education*, 60(1), 99–122.

Miller, G. A. (1956). The magical number seven, plus or minus two: Some limits on our capacity for processing information. *Psychological Review*, 63(2), 81.

Squire, L. R. (2009). The legacy of patient HM for neuroscience. *Neuron*, 61(1), 6–9.

Suzuki, W. A. (2007). Making new memories: The role of the hippocampus in new associative learning. *Annals of the New York Academy of Sciences*, 1097(1), 1–11.

Sweller, J. (1994). Cognitive load theory, learning difficulty, and instructional design. *Learning and Instruction* 4(4), 295–312.

Weinstein, Y., Sumeracki, M., & Caviglioli, O. (2018). *Understanding how we learn: A visual guide.* Routledge.

5 Neuroplasticity

London Taxi Drivers

One of the most challenging tests in the world is the one that Transport for London requires for all aspiring London taxi drivers. To become an officially licensed London driver, applicants must demonstrate the ability to get from point A to B with maximum efficiency. But this far exceeds what GPS technology can do, as there are tens of thousands of streets in London, and to further complicate matters, applicants must be able to identify landmarks and use unofficial streets as well. And they must do all this while simultaneously considering a variety of factors such as the day and time, anticipated traffic, possible alternative routes, and many others. For each of these reasons, it takes years of driving and studying the London streets in preparation for the test for the elite few who do ultimately pass.

Dr. Eleanor Maguire, a neuroscientist at University College London, and her team researched the brains of London taxi drivers both before and after studying for the test. Using magnetic resonance imaging (MRI), her research team discovered that the hippocampus of the taxi driver applicants grew in volume as a result of their intense study of the layout and routes of London streets required to pass the license exam (Maguire et al., 2000; Maguire et al., 2006). Dr. Maguire and her team's fascinating research demonstrated that the human brain indeed grows and changes in response to intense training and use.

Unpacking Neuroplasticity

As demonstrated through research, the human brain's structure and function are not fixed; rather, they are highly adaptable. As we learned in Chapter 4, if a person practices something enough, their brain will repurpose neurons to help with the task even if those neurons already have another job to do. Additionally, the brain can also reroute neurons so that otherwise unused areas are put to work. For example, the part of the brain responsible for vision still works for blind people, however it is used for other sensory purposes, just not sight. So in the truest sense, it is possible to shape the brain in the ways that we desire through conscious, deliberate effort, training, and use. In the previous chapter, I briefly defined neuroplasticity as the brain's ability to adapt and change through the strengthening or weakening of neural connections, or the growth of new neurons altogether. But to truly be strong practitioners, it is important that we unpack at greater depth exactly what neuroplasticity consists of and how it occurs, so that we can optimize for it.

What Is Neuroplasticity?

As discussed in the previous chapter, all of us are born with a nervous system (i.e. brain and neurons) which is designed to adapt, change, and be customized. When we are young, our

DOI: 10.4324/9781003593607-7

nervous system takes in the outside world and develops at a very fast rate. As we grow, some neural connections grow stronger, while others change or are removed because they do not serve us well. We call this process *learning*. In this way, the young brain is a learning machine; or worded differently, the young brain is extremely "plastic." In fact, for children and adolescents, mere exposure to sensory input is enough to learn from it. This phase of learning passively with minimal effort lasts until approximately the age 25. The adage that "Neurons that fire together, wire together" is true, particularly in the first 25 years of development. But this process does not work the same way once reaching adulthood (Knowland & Thomas, 2014).

After this point, the human brain is designed to then rely on the foundation of neural connections formed during the first two decades of life. As Knowland and Thomas (2014) point out:

> Too much brain plasticity in adulthood would result in information having to be constantly relearned. In a sense, the brain gambles that the current neural environment *(at age ~25)* will be the relevant one throughout (the remainder of the) individual's life.
>
> (Knowland & Thomas, 2014, pp. 102–103)

And it is for this neuroscientific fact that we distinguish between andragogy and pedagogy.

The Truth of Neurogenesis

After puberty, the human brain and nervous system adds relatively few new neurons. It is true that research has shown evidence of neurogenesis in the adult brain; however, this is an extremely small number of new neurons compared to what occurs in early development. Therefore, because neurogenesis makes up so little of neuroplasticity in the adult brain, neuroplasticity is therefore most accurately described as a *strengthening of* existing neural connections or *removal of* preexisting neural connections. The neurogenesis element of neuroplasticity is the less common element.

Neuroplasticity in Adults

After age 25, adults must engage in a different set of processes to experience changes in our nervous system, and then have those changes remain or "stick." (It is because of this fact that I was explicit in Chapter 1 in saying that in this book we are focusing on andragogy.) Unlike the ease and passivity of learning before the age of 25, focused attention is required for an adult. Specifically, the desire to learn something new or the recognition of something—cognitive, behavioral, or socioemotional—that is intrinsically motivating for someone to learn is the first step of adult neuroplasticity. Figure 5.1 below captures the full

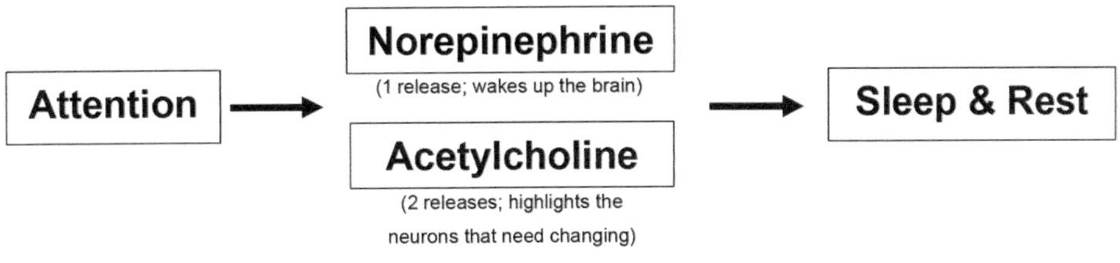

Figure 5.1 Adult neuroplasticity

mechanism that triggers neuroplasticity in adults. Note that children do not need to have this desire or recognition, because the plasticity of the child brain is always flipped on. But as adults we must be intentional to manually turn the switch on. Recognizing that we want to learn something is what turns our adult brain switch on.

This phenomenon is the same throughout the entire adult lifespan. In fact, fascinating research looking at hundreds of thousands MRI scans, across over 100 studies, from over 100,000 participants has revealed evidence of neuroplasticity into the ninth decade of life (i.e. into one's nineties) (Bethlehem et al., 2022). So, in the truest sense, we can teach an old dog new tricks.

The Triggers of Neuroplasticity

Neuroplasticity can be ***adaptive***, meaning your neurons can rewire to allow you to do things you could not do before: do better, think better, feel better, etc. Neuroplasticity can also be ***maladaptive***, which refers to changes in the brain in response to repeated exposure to an experience that is either stressful, traumatic, or from an injury. Maladaptive neuroplasticity leads to changes in the way the brain functions, which can in turn impact a person's ability to cope with future stress and psychological trauma. For our purposes however, we will focus on the adaptive type of neuroplasticity. The moment an adult is aware of making some change and attention is given to that change, neurochemicals are released in the brain which stamp down particular behaviors, thoughts, or emotional patterns that tell the rest of the nervous system, "This is the change we want to make." So in this sense, when we want to make a change it all starts with focused attention, and that attention is precisely what opens up neuroplasticity to those specific experiences. Specifically, when we pay careful attention there are two neurochemicals that are released from multiple sites in our brain that highlight the neural circuits that might need changing: ***norepinephrine*** and ***acetylcholine***. It is not a guarantee that there will be neural change, but it is the first milestone that must be passed. To explore neuroplasticity thoroughly, I will first unpack adult attention, followed by the two neurochemicals that are released as a result, norepinephrine and acetylcholine. We will lastly consider the final pieces of neuroplasticity: sleep and rest.

Attention

Akin to working out at the gym, adult attention is a mental muscle. Research at Emory University (Desbordes et al., 2012) revealed that a trick for strengthening one's ability to focus was not in keeping attention locked on one thing over extended time; rather, it was in continuously bringing the focus/attention back when the mind did stray. This occurs because the adult brain is meant to economize attention, which is why when we do the same thing repeatedly, we begin to not recognize things. Think about driving to work, where you have the same route day after day, year after year. After a while, you stop noticing things as your mind is able to wonder because you know the route so well. As I will discuss further later in this chapter, when the brain sees something new or novel, it becomes excited.

Additionally, Dr. Andrew Huberman, a neuroscientist at Stanford University's School of Medicine, explained this fundamental principle: "mental focus follows visual focus. In blind people, mental focus follows auditory focus" (Huberman, 2021). For those with eyesight, our brains give attention to whatever our eyes are focused on. Extending this idea further, there are three specific altitudes of attention that I will refer to as Levels A, B, and C (Goleman, 2013).

The top level, *Level A*, is what we consider optimal attention and focus. At the top level, a person's focus is 100%. There are no distractions and, interestingly, it feels good to be in this zone. In the psychology literature, this level of attention and focus is referred to as "flow."

A person is in the middle level, *Level B*, if he or she has too much to do, with too little time. The science of this level is referred to as the "*neurobiology of frazzle*." At this level there is a steady amount of stress. The person cannot stop thinking about what is stressing him/her. This level is not close to optimal focus (Level A), where a person can focus clearly on the task at-hand. It is in this Level B where a person is susceptible to allowing emotions to take over their attention.

The lowest altitude of attention is Level C, where the individual is undermotivated and disengaged. To be clear, mind-wandering can be extremely valuable. In fact, periods of reflection and creativity are necessary for innovative thinking. Creative ideas and innovative solutions often arise when you are in the shower, driving to work, walking the dog, or simply daydreaming. This phenomenon exists because during mind-wandering we can make connections between remote elements in new and meaningful ways. So, please, do not think mind-wandering is bad in and of itself, for it is certainly not.

But for neuroplasticity to occur, focused attention is required. And we can certainly do things that make it easier for the mind to focus attention. For instance, novelty, humor, and storytelling are research-proven mechanisms by which we can effectively capture and maintain the learner's attention (see Chapter 12). Conversely, we can just as easily do things that make it harder. For example, consider the last mandatory compliance training you took—well, how enjoyable was it?

Another principle of attention is that repetition shapes the adult brain. And there is a two-for-one available here. Practicing focused attention relies on the same neural circuitry that calms stormy emotions. A person's ability to manage emotions is tightly linked to their capacity to focus attention (Wadlinger & Isaacowitz, 2011). We will discuss emotion in greater depth in Chapter 11.

Norepinephrine

The moment we focus our attention, the first chemical release is ***norepinephrine***, which is released by locus coeruleus, a region of the brainstem. In the process of neuroplasticity, the role of norepinephrine is to essentially wake-up the brain. The presence of norepinephrine increases alertness, thereby increasing the amount of information our brains absorb for a period of time. With focused attention and the release of norepinephrine, the prefrontal cortex signals to the rest of the brain that something we are about to experience is worth our full focus. Therefore, plasticity starts with alertness, and alertness originating from our attention can arise out of joy, love, or even fear. No alertness means no neuroplasticity. In this manner, norepinephrine is a necessary chemical precursor for neuroplasticity to occur, but alertness alone is not sufficient to account for how this process unfolds.

Acetylcholine

With norepinephrine released, the second chemical release is ***acetylcholine***, which must be released simultaneously from two sites in the brain: the brainstem and nucleus basalis. The parabrachial region of the brainstem sends an acetylcholine signal to the thalamus which receives sensory inputs from the outside world. Acetylcholine serves as a spotlight by amplifying a person's cone of attention—that is, acetylcholine amplifies the signal coming in while reducing surrounding noise. In addition, the nucleus basalis must send additional acetylcholine to the precise neural location responsible for the desired KSAs, where it marks those exact neurons for change.

To summarize, we need all three releases: one release of norepinephrine and two simultaneous releases of acetylcholine. When all three are stimulated, whatever you happen to be paying attention to, listening to, or doing then immediately takes over the mental representation in the brain. When all three are present, a person's neural connections will most certainly change. But all three are required: the nervous system only changes when the key neurochemicals (i.e. acetylcholine and norepinephrine) are released and allow the relevant neuronal connections to strengthen or weaken.

On this point, a misconception exists in pop culture and social media: that every experience changes our brain. A simple search on YouTube will produce a number of speakers who state, "*Your brain is going to be different after this lecture.*" But this is absolutely not true for adults. The nervous system only changes when the key neurochemicals (i.e. acetylcholine and norepinephrine) are released and allow the relevant neuronal connections to strengthen or weaken. Just because you and I may be listening to a person speak, does not necessarily mean our brain is fazed in the least.

Sleep and Non-sleep Deep Rest

Thus far, the processes described above represent only the *trigger* to neuroplasticity. Because while neuroplasticity is initiated by focused attention when we are awake, the actual neural rewiring takes place when we are in a state of sleep or non-sleep deep rest (e.g. meditation, reflection) (Gilley, 2023). When an adult focuses on something, that night and subsequent nights while you are sleeping, the neural circuits that were highlighted (or "stamped") with acetylcholine will strengthen, while others will weaken or be lost. Remember that the acetylcholine provides a stamp on the brain by neurochemically marking those synapses which are then primed to change while we are asleep or resting. But the kicker is that sleep is anything but a period of inactivity; rather, sleep is a critical time in which the brain revisits past moments and recodes the experiences and knowledge acquired during the day. Therefore, mastering sleep is key to reinforce the learning that occurs. An adult must get sleep.

There is also one way to partially supplement or bypass the need for deep sleep, and that is through *non-sleep deep rest* (NSDR). Research shows that post-training meditation, shallow naps, and yoga can have the same neural effect as during deep sleep, because there is a rapid replay of what was just learned, just like during sleep (Doinova, 2022). Research has found that from taking a 20 minute nap, eyes closed with minimal/no sensory input, the rates of learning are significantly higher for the information learned than if the individual only had a good night of sleep (Eichenlaub et al., 2020). This is further magnified when rest (10 second pauses) happens during training (referred to as "inter-practice rest") because you are allowing time for the neural circuits to reorder themselves, which is the basis for learning. This suggests that there is an advantage to letting the mind rest after significant episodes of learning.

To illustrate this idea, we look at the words of Arnold Samuelson, who was a farm boy from South Dakota in his early twenties in 1934, with dreams of becoming a writer. He read a short story in the *New York Times* written by Ernest Hemingway that captivated his mind so much that he determined that he had to meet the author. So he hunted down Mr. Hemingway to Key West, Florida, where he was living at the time. When Samuelson asked what advice he might share to a young aspiring writer such as himself, Hemingway shared the following advice:

> "The most important thing I've learned about writing is that you should never write too much at once," Hemingway said, touching my arm with his finger. "You never

> have to do it in one sitting. Leave some for the next day. The most important thing is knowing when to stop. When you start writing and everything is going well, come to an interesting place and when you know what is going to happen next, that is the time to stop. Then you have to leave it as it is and not think about it; let it rest and your subconscious mind do the rest. The next morning, when you've had a good sleep and you've rested, rewrite what you wrote the day before until you get to the interesting place where you knew what was going to happen next. Write again and repeat the sequence again, leaving it at the next interesting point. And so on. That way, your subject will always be full of interesting places. It's the way to write a novel that never stalls and is interesting as you go along."
>
> (Samuelson, 1988)

It should come as no surprise that an author with the experience and legacy as Hemingway was keenly aware of the idea that the mind, like a muscle, needs rest to perform optimally.

Reflection and Meditation

In our discussion of the role of rest—specifically, NSDR—to kickstart the neuroplasticity process before night sleep, we must also consider the specific acts of *reflection* and *meditation*. Research shows that reflection is a central feature of the encoding process and serves the function of solidifying the connection between what a learner experiences and the meaning/learning that they derive from that experience (Denton, 2011; Helyer, 2015; Smith & Martin, 2014).

Research has also shown cognitive and memory improvement for those who regularly meditate (Guidotti et al., 2021). Basso et al. (2019) compared individuals who meditated 12 minutes per day against a control group who did not meditate. They discovered that the meditation group's focus on the present moment served to calm the people down (i.e. reduced stress) which set them up for cognitive success for the rest of their day. (See also Austin & Laprinzi (2019) for additional research on the positive effects of meditation on memory/recall.)

Optimizing Our Neuroplasticity

It is important to note that patterns of neuroplasticity vary highly both *between* people and *within* people when learning different skills. As a result, there is no one-size-fits all approach to learning or training. In fact, the notion of the "average learner" is talked about by CAST—the creators of Universal Design for Learning—as a counterproductive concept. In this manner, designing for the "average learner" is always an unwise approach.

We know that norepinephrine is required for our brain's readiness for neuroplasticity. It is also true that a good night's sleep and some caffeine can help with this. But there are several alternative mechanisms that research has also shown cause the release of norepinephrine. For example, employing your friends to keep you accountable to accomplish a goal, is one shame-based way that can work. Another is to do something out of love or joy: "I'm doing X because I'm devoting it to someone." For norepinephrine release, however, it really does not matter the source or motivating factor. That is, it does not matter if a person is focused out of fear or love or any other reason.

The best way to get better at focusing is to use the mechanisms of focus that you were born with. The key principle here is that mental focus follows visual focus (think: your mind follows your eyes). Focus in the brain is anchored to our visual system. Therefore, the key is to focus visually, to heighten our mental focus. The focus protocols we want are

those that give us a greater *depth* and *duration* of focus. When we are relaxed and our eyes wander the room, we are passively taking in the sensory input of the room around us and cognitively there is not much happening. But when our eyes move inward toward a target, our field of vision narrows, and our focus activates a neuronal pathway in our brainstem that triggers the release of norepinephrine and acetylcholine at the relevant sites in the brain for neuroplasticity to occur. So, if you want to have a strong mental focus, it is important to first practice visual focus.

Conversely, suppose you want to sharpen your auditory focus. Closing your eyes is one way to do so. Regardless of the bio-hacks you may take, when it comes to increasing our attention and readiness to learn, it is more effective to do so *before* the learning experience occurs—anything to increase the level of alertness. For example, if you want to enhance your alertness and attention, consider taking an ice cold shower before a learning experience—research has shown that cold exposure can lead to a slow-drip adrenaline release for up to 4 hours (Leppäluoto et al., 2008).

The Role of Neurochemicals

Dopamine

Dopamine is a neurotransmitter that research has shown controls human motivation and reinforcement (i.e. feelings of "wanting"). Dopamine also impacts human reward and pleasure (or feelings of "liking"). But to be crystal clear, dopamine controls our motivation much more than it does our feelings of pleasure. Not surprisingly, dopamine is associated with memory.

First, dopamine helps in focusing attention on important stimuli and encoding information into memory. When an individual engages in a behavior that leads to a rewarding experience, dopamine is released, strengthening the neural connections associated with that behavior. This reinforcement enhances the likelihood of repeating the behavior in the future. Second, dopamine is also involved in motor learning, influencing the development of new motor skills and the refinement of existing ones. In certain brain regions, such as the basal ganglia, dopamine helps regulate the planning and execution of movements, contributing to the learning and mastery of motor tasks.

Oxytocin

There is evidence to suggest that oxytocin may influence certain aspects of learning and memory, particularly those related to social interactions and emotional experiences. Oxytocin is released most strongly at two occasions: by a mother when she has a newborn; and during sexual intimacy. As far as learning is concerned, oxytocin is often referred to as the "love hormone" or "bonding hormone" because it is released in response to social interactions, especially positive and affiliative ones. It is associated with feelings of trust and bonding. Positive social interactions are known to influence learning, particularly in the context of social information. Studies suggest that oxytocin may enhance the encoding and retrieval of socially relevant and emotionally salient information, potentially impacting learning in social contexts, including social cues and norms (Clark-Elford et al., 2014; Engelmann et al., 1996).

Research has also discovered that oxytocin is released when we receive instruction or advice from experts. Specifically, Xu et al. (2019) found that oxytocin can increase acceptance of social advice given by individual experts without influencing their perceived trustworthiness. Oxytocin was found to also enhance the impact of information provided by said experts.

Serotonin

Serotonin is a neurotransmitter found in the brain and gastrointestinal tract. It is historically known to impact a person's mood, sleep, and the digestion process. But serotonin has also been linked to memory. Serotonin is involved in the modulation of memory formation, particularly in the hippocampus, the brain region critical for the consolidation of declarative memories. Research suggests that serotonin can influence synaptic plasticity, thus *strengthening the memory* of a learned event (Teixeira et al., 2018). Additionally, evidence suggests that serotonin increases the *speed* at which adults learn new information (Iigaya et al., 2018). Lastly, recent research has found that prolonged boosting of serotonin particularly helps a person learn from mistakes (Michely et al., 2022).

The Role of Exercise

There are multiple benefits to exercise, ranging from short-term to long-term. Beginning with the short-term effects of exercise, research has demonstrated that exercise boosts our mood by decreasing anxiety, depression, and hostility. Findings also suggest that exercise leads to feelings of increased energy that last up to 2 hours. But beyond that, there are specific *learning* benefits to exercise including improved prefrontal function (e.g. focused attention on tasks), and significant improvements in cognitive motor response time.

Perhaps most importantly, exercise triggers a neurochemical bath to the hippocampus. Over time, this consistent showering of neurochemicals causes an individual's hippocampus to grow larger in size, while increasing the overall capacity and capability of the hippocampus (e.g. greater ability to form new memories) (Basso & Suzuki, 2017).

What Makes Things Memorable

There are four key attributes that make something memorable: novelty, repetition, emotional resonance, and association (Huberman, 2022). I unpack these four next.

Novelty

Our brains are drawn to something new. New things, different things, and counterintuitive things, all attract our attention with ease. Novelty activates the amygdala to increase sensorial perception. Additionally, novelty promotes dopamine release, which improves motivation and activates reward processes (Schomaker & Meeter, 2015; Schomaker et al., 2014). Each of these effects directly and indirectly contribute to learning and memory improvement. In fact, research by Ballarini et al. (2013) revealed that learners exposed to novelty demonstrate better memory than those taught the same material but without the novelty.

Repetition

You may have heard the adage, "Repetition is a law of learning" (Hinckley, 2000). Well, it is absolutely true. Our brains better remember seeing, doing, or feeling the same thing repeatedly. Research by Zhan et al. (2018) found that compared to learning a concept in a single event, learning the concept in six events led to stronger activation in the hippocampus. In terms of neuroplasticity, the fundamental fact exists that focused repetition strengthens the neural connections related to the KSA being repeated. After only five chapters thus far of this book, have you noticed that I have already discussed several concepts multiple times? Well, this is not an accident.

Emotional Resonance

Some memories can bypass the need for repetition. We refer to such events as "flashbulb memories" (or "one-trial learning"), where a person vividly remembers an experience after only a single occurrence. While I discuss the role of emotions on learning more in Chapter 11, I will state here that the adult brain is skewed to remember more details from emotionally-charged experiences, particularly those with a *negative* orientation (Rozin & Royzman, 2001). Why is that? Because as a survival mechanism, the human mind is always on the lookout for potentially harmful, dangerous, or threatening experiences.

Additionally, we easily remember the happiest, saddest, and funny moments of our lives. This is due to both the amygdala and hippocampus. Recall that our amygdala processes emotion, especially in situations that are either threatening or surprising. The amygdala specifically helps the hippocampus work more efficiently in the face of the threatening/surprising situation by rapidly encoding those memories into the brain. The hippocampus, in turn, further consolidates those initial *memory traces* into long-term memory, and helps to build association (think: pine tree smell and Christmas season). Besides memory consolidation, the hippocampus also supports the prefrontal cortex in its efforts to combine new and old information to form novel schemas (Gilboa & Marlatte, 2017), which is especially the case for emotionally resonant memories.

Association

Associative learning is the psychological concept that reflects learning that occurs when two unrelated elements (e.g. objects, sights, sounds, ideas) become connected in our brains. It should come as no surprise that it is easier to remember something when the associations are strong or high. That is, it is easy to remember something when there is a significant overlap in associations. For example, it is easier to remember a new acquaintance when the two of you share many mutual friends. The corollary is also true: it is more challenging to remember something when there are minimal to no associations.

Application of This Chapter

The initial trigger to neuroplasticity is *focused attention*. Therefore, as a professional it is prudent to take steps to ensure the greatest likelihood of focused attention for the learners. Distractions should be minimal; communication should be clear and direct. Also, we should always avoid conditions that might lead to cognitive overload. When our working memory is overly taxed, no amount of focused attention can compensate. Thus, it is critical to always be thoughtful and deliberate with the *amount* and *complexity* of information being presented to the learner.

Additionally, research has shown that novelty, repetition, emotional resonance, and association each enhance the memorability of any information or experience. Therefore, to address *novelty*, consider introducing a topic or concept with counterintuitive or illustrative anecdotes. New and surprising stimuli can engage the brain and trigger neuroplasticity, as the brain adapts to new information. Regarding *repetition*, presenting a complex concept multiple times is superior to a single dose. Therefore, consider deploying mechanisms by which a complex concept can be introduced in multiple instances spread out over time, thus achieving spaced repetition into the curriculum. Revisiting and reviewing material over time helps strengthen synaptic connections and reinforces memory. For *emotional resonance*, connect learning to emotions and personal experiences. This type of engagement can stimulate the release of neurochemicals that enhance memory and learning. (I will

discuss the role of emotions in learning in greater depth in Chapter 7.) Lastly, regarding *association*, it is advantageous to introduce complex topics using something familiar to the learner. It is therefore always wise for a practitioner to understand and leverage the prior knowledge of learners. Further, identifying an illustrative example or application of a topic is one way to help learners make associations.

References

Austin, M., & Loprinzi, P. D. (2019). Acute exercise and mindfulness meditation on learning and memory: Randomized controlled intervention. *Health Promotion Perspectives*, 9(4), 314.

Ballarini, F., Martínez, M. C., Díaz Perez, M., Moncada, D., & Viola, H. (2013). Memory in elementary school children is improved by an unrelated novel experience. *PloS one*, 8(6), e66875.

Basso, J. C., McHale, A., Ende, V., Oberlin, D. J., & Suzuki, W. A. (2019). Brief, daily meditation enhances attention, memory, mood, and emotional regulation in non-experienced meditators. *Behavioural Brain Research*, 356, 208–220.

Basso, J. C., & Suzuki, W. A. (2017). The effects of acute exercise on mood, cognition, neurophysiology, and neurochemical pathways: A review. *Brain Plasticity*, 2(2), 127–152.

Bethlehem, R. A., Seidlitz, J., White, S. R., Vogel, J. W., Anderson, K. M., Adamson, C., Adler, S., Alexopoulos, G. S., Anagnostou, E., Areces-Gonzalez, A. and Astle, D. E. (2022). Brain charts for the human lifespan. *Nature*, 604(7906), 525–533.

Clark-Elford, R., Nathan, P. J., Auyeung, B., Voon, V., Sule, A., Müller, U., ... & Baron-Cohen, S. (2014). The effects of oxytocin on social reward learning in humans. *International Journal of Neuropsychopharmacology*, 17(2), 199–209.

Denton, D. (2011). Reflection and learning: Characteristics, obstacles, and implications. *Educational Philosophy and Theory*, 43(8), 838–852.

Desbordes, G., Negi, L. T., Pace, T. W., Wallace, B. A., Raison, C. L., & Schwartz, E. L. (2012). Effects of mindful-attention and compassion meditation training on amygdala response to emotional stimuli in an ordinary, non-meditative state. *Frontiers in Human Neuroscience*, 6, 292.

Doinova, G. (2022). Neuroplasticity induced by meditation practices: A systematic review. Thesis, University of Skövde.

Eichenlaub, J. B., Jarosiewicz, B., Saab, J., Franco, B., Kelemen, J., Halgren, E., ... & Cash, S. S. (2020). Replay of learned neural firing sequences during rest in human motor cortex. *Cell Reports*, 31(5).

Engelmann, M., Twotjak, C., Neumann, I., Ludwig, M., & Landgraf, R. (1996). Behavioral consequences of intracerebral vasopressin and oxytocin: Focus on learning and memory. *Neuroscience & Biobehavioral Reviews*, 20(3), 341–358.

Gilboa, A., & Marlatte, H. (2017). Neurobiology of schemas and schema-mediated memory. *Trends in cognitive sciences*, 21(8), 618–631.

Gilley, R. R. (2023). The role of sleep in cognitive function: The value of a good night's rest. *Clinical EEG and Neuroscience*, 54(1), 12–20.

Goleman, D. (2013). Daniel Goleman on focus: The secret to high performance and fulfilment [Video]. www.youtube.com/watch?v=HTfYv3IEOqM.

Guidotti, R., Del Gratta, C., Perrucci, M. G., Romani, G. L., & Raffone, A. (2021). Neuroplasticity within and between functional brain networks in mental training based on long-term meditation. *Brain Sciences*, 11(8), 1086.

Helyer, R. (2015). Learning through reflection: The critical role of reflection in work-based learning (WBL). *Journal of Work-Applied Management*, 7(1), 15–27.

Hinckley, G. B. (2000). Great shall be the peace of thy children. www.churchofjesuschrist.org/study/general-conference/2000/10/great-shall-be-the-peace-of-thy-children?lang=eng.

Huberman, A. (Host). (2021). How your nervous system works and changes. [Video podcast episode]. www.youtube.com/watch?v=H-XfCl-HpRM.

Huberman, A. (Host). (2022). Boost attention & memory with science-based tools [Video podcast episode]. www.youtube.com/watch?v=099hgtRoUZw.

Knowland, V. C., & Thomas, M. S. (2014). Educating the adult brain: How the neuroscience of learning can inform educational policy. *International Review of Education*, 60(1), 99–122.

Kuo, M. F., Grosch, J., Fregni, F., Paulus, W., & Nitsche, M. A. (2007). Focusing effect of acetylcholine on neuroplasticity in the human motor cortex. *Journal of Neuroscience*, 27(52), 14442–14447.

Leppäluoto, J., Westerlund, T., Huttunen, P., Oksa, J., Smolander, J., Dugué, B., & Mikkelsson, M. (2008). Effects of long-term whole-body cold exposures on plasma concentrations of ACTH, beta-endorphin, cortisol, catecholamines and cytokines in healthy females. *Scandinavian Journal of Clinical and Laboratory Investigation*, 68(2), 145–153.

Iigaya, K., Fonseca, M. S., Murakami, M., Mainen, Z. F., & Dayan, P. (2018). An effect of serotonergic stimulation on learning rates for rewards apparent after long intertrial intervals. *Nature Communications*, 9(1), 2477.

Maguire, E. A., Gadian, D. G., Johnsrude, I. S., Good, C. D., Ashburner, J., Frackowiak, R. S., & Frith, C. D. (2000). Navigation-related structural change in the hippocampi of taxi drivers. *Proceedings of the National Academy of Sciences*, 97(8), 4398–4403.

Maguire, E. A., Woollett, K., & Spiers, H. J. (2006). London taxi drivers and bus drivers: A structural MRI and neuropsychological analysis. *Hippocampus*, 16(12), 1091–1101.

Michely, J., Eldar, E., Erdman, A., Martin, I. M., & Dolan, R. J. (2022). Serotonin modulates asymmetric learning from reward and punishment in healthy human volunteers. *Communications Biology*, 5(1), 812.

Rozin, P., & Royzman, E. B. (2001). Negativity bias, negativity dominance, and contagion. *Personality and Social Psychology Review*, 5(4), 296–320.

Samuelson, A. (1988). *With Hemingway: A year in Key West and Cuba*. Henry Holt & Co.

Schomaker, J., & Meeter, M. (2015). Short-and long-lasting consequences of novelty, deviance and surprise on brain and cognition. *Neuroscience & Biobehavioral Reviews*, 55, 268–279.

Schomaker, J., van Bronkhorst, M. L., & Meeter, M. (2014). Exploring a novel environment improves motivation and promotes recall of words. *Frontiers in Psychology*, 5, 918.

Smith, S., & Martin, J. (2014). Practitioner capability: Supporting critical reflection during work based placement–a pilot study. *Higher Education Skills and Work-Based Learning*, 4(3), 284–300.

Teixeira, C. M., Rosen, Z. B., Suri, D., Sun, Q., Hersh, M., Sargin, D., ... & Ansorge, M. S. (2018). Hippocampal 5-HT input regulates memory formation and Schaffer collateral excitation. *Neuron*, 98(5), 992–1004.

Wadlinger, H. A., & Isaacowitz, D. M. (2011). Fixing our focus: Training attention to regulate emotion. *Personality and Social Psychology Review*, 15(1), 75–102.

Xu, L., Becker, B., & Kendrick, K. M. (2019). Oxytocin facilitates social learning by promoting conformity to trusted individuals. *Frontiers in Neuroscience*, 13, 56.

Zhan, L., Guo, D., Chen, G., & Yang, J. (2018). Effects of repetition learning on associative recognition over time: Role of the hippocampus and prefrontal cortex. *Frontiers in Human Neuroscience*, 12, 277.

6 Metacognition and Related Learning Theories

Metacognition

Metacognition is often described as "thinking about thinking." However, there is much more nuance involved. "Metacognition—the ability to know oneself, to self-evaluate, to mentally simulate what would happen if we acted this way or that way—plays a fundamental role in human learning" (Dehaene, 2021, p. 23). Metacognition refers to the self-awareness and understanding of how one thinks, learns, solve problems, make decisions, and manages cognitive tasks. Metacognition encompasses a range of cognitive processes related to self-awareness and self-regulation of one's mental activities, and it also includes all the cognitive processes and strategies that regulate and enhance the learning process (Livingston, 2003). As a result, metacognition is less of a single, standalone learning theory, per se; instead, it is better to consider metacognition more of a macro body of work that describes how learning becomes knowledge and what mental factors influence whether that knowledge leads to lasting behavioral change. We will next consider the two main components of metacognition—*knowledge* and *control.*

Metacognitive Knowledge

Metacognitive knowledge involves awareness and understanding of various aspects of your cognitive processes. Specifically, metacognitive knowledge includes knowledge about: (1) your own cognitive strengths and weaknesses; (2) different learning strategies and when to use them for your own optimal learning; (3) the nature of the task at hand and the strategies that might be most effective for it; and (4) the goals and objectives of your thinking or learning process.

Cognitive Strengths and Weaknesses

Metacognition is the cognitive process that enables individuals to become aware of their own cognitive strengths and weaknesses. This awareness, in turn, informs their decision-making, learning strategies, and problem-solving approaches. Awareness of one's own cognitive strengths and weaknesses is an essential component of self-awareness and self-regulation, leading to more effective and adaptive cognitive functioning.

Metacognition also involves monitoring one's own cognitive processes, such as problem-solving, decision-making, and learning. By actively observing and analyzing how you approach various tasks, you can gain insight into your cognitive strengths and weaknesses. Metacognitive awareness of one's own cognitive strengths and weaknesses is crucial for effective learning and problem-solving. Such awareness allows individuals to tailor their approaches to maximize strengths and mitigate weaknesses, leading to improved outcomes.

DOI: 10.4324/9781003593607-8

Over time, through metacognition, individuals begin to recognize patterns in their cognitive abilities. They notice areas where they consistently perform well and areas where they may struggle or encounter challenges. Further, metacognition often involves goal setting, and individuals may set learning or performance goals that reflect their desire to leverage their strengths and address their weaknesses. These goals are based on their self-awareness of their cognitive attributes.

Understanding one's cognitive strengths and weaknesses through metacognition can also impact *self-efficacy*, which is an individual's belief in their ability to accomplish a task (Bandura, 1977, 1986, 1997). This self-awareness can lead to increased confidence in areas of strength, as well as a commitment to improving (i.e. exerting the effort required to improve) in areas of weakness.

Deploying Different Learning Strategies

As part of metacognition, individuals assess the effectiveness of the strategies they use in different cognitive tasks. This evaluation helps in identifying which strategies play to their strengths and which ones reveal weaknesses. Individuals can then distinguish which learning strategies to deploy in which situations, for which topics, at which times, to optimize their own learning.

The Nature of Tasks and Determining Best Strategies

Metacognition and the nature of the task are closely intertwined because metacognition allows individuals to assess the task's specific requirements, choose the most effective strategies, plan for their implementation, and adapt as needed. This adaptability is critical for optimizing cognitive performance and achieving desired outcomes in various tasks and problem-solving situations.

Metacognition first involves analyzing the nature of the task at hand (i.e. task analysis). This means understanding the requirements, objectives, and challenges associated with the task. Experts understand that different tasks may require different cognitive processes and strategies for success. Then based on the analysis of the task, individuals engage in metacognitive thinking to select the most appropriate strategies. They draw upon their knowledge of effective learning and problem-solving strategies to determine which approaches are likely to yield the best results for the specific task.

During the execution of the task, metacognition involves self-monitoring. Expert individuals continuously assess their progress and the effectiveness of the chosen strategies in light of the task's demands. This monitoring helps them make real-time adjustments if necessary. The recognition of the nature of the task and the strategies that are most effective often leads to task-specific adaptation. This means that individuals adjust their cognitive approaches, based on their metacognitive awareness, to better align with the unique requirements of each task.

Metacognition also allows for the transfer of knowledge and strategies between different tasks. When individuals recognize the commonalities or patterns across tasks, they can apply strategies that have been successful in one context to another, as long as it's appropriate. Further, the interplay between metacognition and the task's nature directly impacts efficiency and effectiveness. When individuals are able to match strategies with the demands of a task, they are more likely to achieve their goals efficiently and successfully.

The Goals and Objectives of Your Thinking/Learning

Obviously, you and I want to ensure that the time and energy we devote to thinking and learning are worth our time and energy expenditure. Therefore, metacognition serves as the

self-regulatory process that ensures that your cognitive activities are purposeful and goal-directed, ultimately leading to more effective learning and problem-solving. In this manner, metacognition involves setting, monitoring, evaluating, adjusting, and reflecting on one's own thinking and learning goals. These goals provide direction and purpose for your cognitive effort and activities.

Metacognition allows you to align your cognitive efforts with your goals and objectives. It ensures that the strategies and activities you choose are in line with what you want to achieve. Metacognition also involves continuous monitoring of your progress toward your goals and objectives. You assess how well you are doing, whether you are on track, and whether any adjustments are necessary. As part of metacognition, you critically evaluate the strategies you are using to accomplish your goals. This includes considering whether the strategies are effective and whether they need modification. Metacognition is also a key component of self-regulation, which means that you actively manage your thinking and learning process to reach your goals. This self-regulation involves making informed decisions about how to achieve your objectives.

After completing a learning or thinking process, metacognition enables you to reflect on whether you achieved your goals and objectives. This reflection allows you to understand what worked well and what needs improvement. Metacognition does not end with the completion of one learning or thinking task; rather, it informs future goal setting by helping you assess your past experiences and determine what you want to achieve next.

It is important to point out that the relationship between metacognition and goals ensures that your cognitive efforts are *efficient* and *effective*. By aligning your thinking and learning with specific objectives, you maximize the likelihood of success. In a related manner, metacognition can also impact your *motivation* and *engagement* in the learning process. Clearly articulated goals and objectives, when recognized and appreciated through metacognition, can enhance a person's commitment to the task.

Metacognitive Control

Metacognitive control involves using your metacognitive knowledge to regulate and control your cognitive processes. Specifically, this includes self-regulation of the following three cognitive processes: (1) planning; (2) reflection; and (3) adjusting.

Planning

Planning consists of goal setting, deciding on strategies, and organizing your approach to a task. For example, imagine you are preparing for a cross-country trip that will have you traveling through various biomes, each with its unique challenges and potential for unforeseen events hampering your progress toward completing this journey. Events like this are inherently exciting for us because they provide opportunities for personal growth and enable us to challenge ourselves in ways we are not often able to in our current circumstances. But consider for a moment, how pleasant or impactful that trip would be if you lacked the proper equipment and resources to see it through to the end. Similar to undertaking a journey, regulating one's own learning also requires proper planning and the right tools to optimize the experience. For learners, planning means understanding what is expected of them from the start, with a syllabus or lesson plan serving as the road map, and the instructor or facilitator as their guide. While you may find the adult learning literature full of various tools and techniques for you to experiment with, for this chapter I will focus on those tools/techniques that deal with memory and the learning strategies can improve learner retention, recall, and overall understanding.

One such technique you may already be familiar with from school and college is *distributed practice*. This method takes advantage of the *spacing effect*, where learners demonstrate a greater recall for information when it is presented to them across several sessions, as opposed to cramming that information into only one or two extended sessions (Dempster, 1989). In fact, so powerful is the difference between spacing learning sessions out versus cramming that it amounts to roughly a doubling of effective learning outcomes (Dempster, 1989).

However, several disagreements exist regarding exactly what length of time during or between sessions learning and retention is maximized (Bradbury, 2016), but for our purposes in workplace learning, it is enough to remind ourselves that learners' attention is limited, sometimes in the manner of seconds (Knudsen, 2007), and that learning is not a one and done process. To sustain long-term behavioral change and performance improvements, learned knowledge must be sustained through frequent recall, similar to how exercising is necessary to sustain muscle growth and development.

Another technique, which you likely have not heard of before, is called retrieval practice. This form of practice takes the idea of learning being akin to exercising a muscle one step further, by making memory recall the method for improving learning, not instruction. If you ever used flashcards to improve your learning, then you have already used retrieval practice in the past. Retrieval practice is based on research relating to the testing effect, where learners consistently demonstrate greater recollection of information after being tested on it (Roediger & Karpicke, 2006), and works by having learners practice actively recalling previous material without referencing learning materials, and then being tested on their current level of recall; not necessarily their level of understanding. Only afterward should students compare the results of the test with the correct information present in their learning materials.

As Karpicke and Blunt (2011) explain, "Not only does retrieval produce learning, but a retrieval event may actually represent a more powerful learning activity than an encoding event." In other words, recalling information is often more effective at improving long-term retention than restudying the same material (Roediger & Butler, 2011). In addition, retrieval practice also appears to be more effective than other popular learning enhancement techniques, such as concept mapping (Karpicke & Blunt (2011). One reason this method is so effective, aside from reinforcing the specific neural circuits that constitute knowledge in the brain through repeated activation (Holtmaat & Svoboda, 2009), is because it enables learners to recognize where they are in the learning process and what gaps exist in their current understanding.

Reflection

Whereas planning concerns what learners and practitioners can do to enhance the learning process *before* applying their skills in a real-world situation, reflection is an inherently *post hoc* process (i.e. after the fact). Reflection involves the act of thinking back on one's experiences and considering what was learned from those experiences. Reflection refers to monitoring your progress, evaluating the effectiveness of your strategies, and assessing your understanding of the significance of an experience. To be clear, reflection is a process of deep thought that can lead to insights and personal growth.

There are certainly also times when reflective practices are best conducted in real-time, we will call this *reflection-in-action* and refers to how an individual approaches a problem (Schön, 1987). This involves how an individual thinks about situations and how to find optimal solutions given certain cues. In the example of a learning experience, the instructor/facilitator evaluates the learners' thinking in the process of an act, through such

methods as think-alouds, and then prompts them to reframe their thinking towards more fruitful or relevant directions of inquiry.

Consider, for instance, the process that medical residents go through during rounds where they may be asked to diagnose a patient or suggest a treatment plan while explaining their reasoning to a senior physician. The purpose of these on-the-job reflective moments is for trainees to practice their ***decision-making process*** while receiving immediate feedback from a more seasoned practitioner, with the experience allowing them to reframe their thought process in a way that will result in a more desirable outcome for the learner and their patients as well. Peter Schön (1987), the progenitor of reflection-in-action, explained it as "thinking like a ___," where the blank is filled in based on profession (e.g. cop, doctor, teacher) (Schön, 1987, p. 39). In this manner, the purpose of the exercise is to transfer the rules of inquiry and decision-making, with applicable knowledge and facts developing deeper over time as they are repeated and combined with further study.

Receiving feedback is another example of a reflective practice, wherein an observer shares their perceptions and knowledge in a way that is relevant to the learner's individual needs, and in a way that provides additional context and information for the receiver to consider when determining their next step in the learning process. However, while we consider feedback as an instance of reflection, it is important to circle back to what *quality feedback* consists of from Chapter 2. Recall that strong feedback provides useful, performance-oriented information for the learner to plan for and practice improved performance, including actual procedural steps for the learner to follow. To be succinct, strong feedback consists of: (1) the ideal state; (2) the current state (from the observer's point of view); and (3) the procedural steps or path to go from the current state to the future state in the most direct, efficient manner possible. When all three elements are present, the receiver of the feedback can then reflect on their performance, envision how to proceed forward toward improved performance. So, while receiving strong feedback is critical for expertise development, it is the person's *reflection* upon receiving the feedback that is most important.

Adjusting

Metacognition serves as the cognitive framework that enables individuals to monitor, evaluate, identify issues, and then make necessary adjustments in their thinking, problem-solving, and learning strategies. The ability to adjust based on metacognitive awareness is a key component of effective learning, decision-making, and problem-solving. To be specific, ***adjusting*** refers to altering or changing your strategies or approach when you realize they are not working—when you need to adapt to new information or new circumstances. This monitoring often leads to the recognition of when adjustments are necessary. For example, you might realize that you are struggling to understand a particular concept, and this awareness prompts you to consider adjusting your approach.

Metacognition enables individuals to identify problems, challenges, or obstacles in their learning or thinking processes. This can include recognizing when a particular strategy is not working effectively or when there is a gap in understanding. Identifying these issues is the first step toward adjusting. Once an individual becomes aware of a problem or challenge through metacognition, you can then use your metacognitive knowledge to adjust your strategies. For example, if a specific study method is not leading to effective learning, you might decide to try a different approach, such as creating flashcards, seeking additional resources, or seeking help from a teacher or tutor.

Additionally, adjusting is a fundamental aspect of self-regulation in learning. Self-regulation involves managing one's learning process, and metacognition plays a critical role in this. When individuals monitor their progress and adjust their strategies based on their

metacognitive assessments, they are effectively self-regulating their learning. The purpose of adjusting, guided by metacognition, is to improve the quality of one's learning or thinking. It involves adapting to the specific demands of a task or problem. Adjusting is a dynamic process where individuals continuously fine-tune their cognitive processes to enhance their performance.

Experiential Learning Theory

Experiential learning is a theory which aligns itself with many of the core tenets of metacognition. Experiential learning theory emphasizes the importance of direct, hands-on experiences as a primary means of learning KSAs. Central to experiential learning is the idea that people learn best when they actively engage with and reflect upon their experiences. Thus, experiential learning is only concerned with the outside world insofar as it facilitates change, or learning, inside the mind. Worded differently, everyone goes through experiences, but the learning benefit only comes to the degree to which reflection of the experience has taken place (Day et al., 2008).

However, you will likely find these distinctions arbitrary and frequently shifting over time. Therefore, practitioners should keep the needs of the learners and the constraints of the training environment at the forefront; please do not feel pressured into pursuing one approach over another out of some form of theoretical obligation or idealogue.

Kolb's Learning Cycle

One of the more critical developments in the history of experiential learning came by way of David Kolb's (2014) four-stage learning cycle (see Figure 6.1 below). The Kolb cycle describes a continuous process where new and unanticipated events compel learners to reconsolidate their thinking to align their expectations with what they experience.

Humans, by nature, strive for equilibrium between our way of rationalizing the world and the realities that we face on a day-to-day basis. When those two misalign, learners experience what is called cognitive dissonance, which describes the sense of discomfort or unease people experience as a result of losing this equilibrium.

Oftentimes learners will first attempt to dismiss the discomfort by attempting to justify their thinking after the fact, such as a smoker justifying their habit by figuring carcinogens are everywhere, so smoking will not impact their health in the grand scheme of things (Festinger, 1957). But when these attempts fail to do away with the contradiction, learners are motivated to construct new logic and thinking to accommodate contradictory evidence and widened perspectives (Elliot & Devine, 1994).

The value of Kolb's work resides in its systematic explanation for how new information goes from the initial perception of contradiction to becoming something that is readily applied to future, real-world circumstances, meaning when it becomes consequential to learners' performance. The learning cycle begins with the concrete experience stage, which occurs when some unexpected experience or outcome results in a conflict between perceptual reality and a learner's preconceived understanding of how things were "supposed" to have occurred.

Once a definite discrepancy between current knowledge and reality is established, the next step is to start thinking about consolidating these two things into one cohesive whole. Kolb refers to this second stage of the cycle as reflective observation, where the learner starts to evaluate divergent explanations that accommodate this new sensorimotor experience and compares them with their current understanding, ultimately determining where their knowledge conflicts with reality.

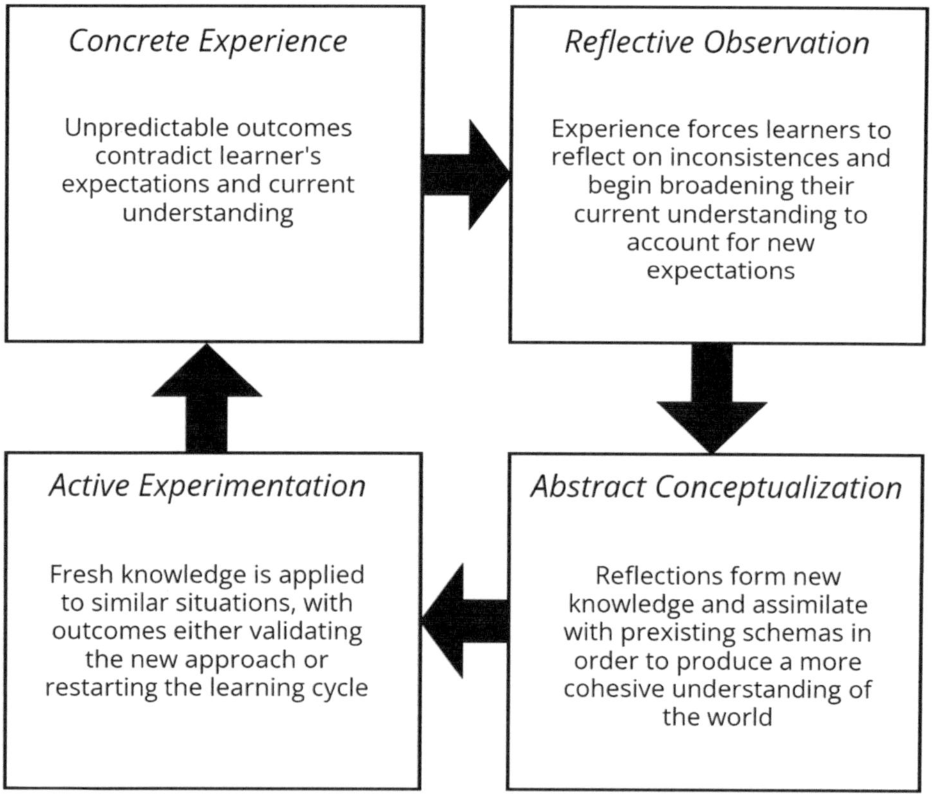

Figure 6.1 Kolb's experiential learning cycle

The third stage, abstract conceptualization, is where that divergent thinking begins to take a more definite shape and assimilates with pre-existing schemas to form a cohesive mental narrative. It is also at this stage the cycle becomes a purely cognitive process, where the initial sensory information from the concrete experience gave way to tentative formulations that have now translated into detailed mental constructs.

Finally, the cycle concludes with active experimentation, where learners are ready to begin applying their new ideas and conceptions to other situations that share similarities with the original experience that kicked off the cycle. Of course, there is no guarantee this new knowledge will work perfectly or even improve the outcome of any subsequent run-ins with this particular set of circumstances, but given time and consistent reflection, it does result in success being notably more likely through each iterative pass of the learning cycle.

Transformational Learning Theory

Another learning theory that is connected to metacognition is transformational learning. According to transformational learning theory, individuals undergo profound and transformative changes in their beliefs, perspectives, and ways of thinking because of their learning experiences. Key features of transformational learning include:

- **Disorienting dilemma:** Transformational learning typically begins with a *disorienting dilemma* or a situation that challenges an individual's existing beliefs, assumptions, or ways of viewing the world. This experience creates cognitive dissonance (i.e. psychological conflict) and prompts individuals to evaluate and question their current perspectives.
- **Self-reflection:** In response to the disorienting dilemma, individuals engage in self-reflection to explore their existing beliefs and how they have been shaped by their past experiences. They examine the assumptions and biases that underlie their thinking.
- **Critical examination:** Transformational learning involves critically examining and questioning one's beliefs and assumptions. This process may involve seeking alternative viewpoints, gathering new information, and engaging in dialogue with others.
- **Perspective transformation:** As individuals engage in self-reflection and critical examination, they may experience a shift in their fundamental perspectives and ways of thinking. This transformation often leads to a more nuanced understanding of the world.
- **Integration of new perspectives:** Transformational learners integrate their newly acquired perspectives into their existing knowledge and belief systems. This integration allows them to make sense of their transformative experiences and apply their new understanding to future situations.
- **Changed behavior:** Transformational learning is not solely a cognitive process; it also involves changes in behavior and action. Individuals who undergo transformational learning are more likely to act in ways that align with their new perspectives and beliefs.

Transformational learning is often associated with adult learners who are motivated to reevaluate their beliefs and values in response to new experiences and changing circumstances. It can have a profound impact on personal development, social and political consciousness, and professional growth.

Application of This Chapter

Without question, metacognition plays a crucial role in learning, problem-solving, decision-making, and overall cognitive development. Individuals with strong metacognitive skills are often more effective learners and problem solvers because they can reflect on their thought processes, identify errors, and make adjustments to improve their performance. In this manner, strong metacognitive skills are tightly associated with expert performance. As discussed in this chapter, both experiential and transformational learning theories have a strong component of reflection and integration of new perspectives. Therefore, in order to best apply the various concepts covered in this chapter, I recommend the following:

1. **Explicitly teach metacognitive strategies:** Design learning experiences and materials that explicitly teach metacognitive strategies to learners. For example, provide guidance on goal setting, planning, monitoring, reflection, and self-evaluation.
2. **Set clear learning objectives:** Clearly articulate learning objectives at the beginning of a course or lesson. This helps learners understand what they are expected to achieve and encourages them to set their own learning goals.
3. **Encourage self-assessment:** Incorporate self-assessment activities, such as quizzes, reflective journals, or self-assessment rubrics, to help learners evaluate their understanding and progress.
4. **Promote reflection:** Design opportunities for reflection into the learning process. Encourage learners to think about their learning experiences, challenges, and strategies for improvement.

5 **Provide feedback:** Offer timely and constructive feedback to help learners understand their strengths and areas for improvement. Encourage them to use this feedback for self-improvement.
6 **Foster goal setting:** Encourage learners to set their own learning goals and objectives. This can be done at the beginning of a course or in response to self-assessment results.
7 **Offer varied learning activities:** Design a variety of learning activities that cater to different metacognitive needs. Some learners may benefit from group discussions, while others may prefer independent research or problem-solving.
8 **Support self-regulation:** Create a learning environment that promotes self-regulation by providing resources, tools, and guidance for time management, study strategies, and organization.
9 **Use metacognitive prompts:** Integrate metacognitive prompts into instructional materials or assignments to encourage learners to think about their thinking. For example, ask questions such as, "What strategies did you use to solve this problem?" or "What could you do differently next time?"
10 **Encourage peer review:** Incorporate peer review processes where learners evaluate and provide feedback on each other's work. This helps them develop metacognitive skills related to assessment and analysis.
11 **Embrace desirable difficulty:** Gradually release responsibility to learners as they develop metacognitive skills. Provide more support initially and then gradually reduce it as they become more independent.
12 **Model metacognitive thinking:** As an instructor or facilitator, model metacognitive thinking by talking through your own thought processes and decision-making during lessons or activities.

By incorporating these principles of metacognition into instructional design and/or learning experience design, professionals can empower learners to take more control of their learning, become more effective problem solvers, and develop skills that extend beyond the specific content being taught. Ultimately, this approach can lead to more engaged and self-directed learners.

References

Bandura, A. (1977). Self-efficacy: Toward a unifying theory of behavioral change. *Psychological Review*, 84(2), 191–215.
Bandura, A. (1986). *Social foundations of thought and action: A social cognitive theory*. Prentice-Hall.
Bandura, A. (1997). *Self-efficacy: The exercise of control*. W. H. Freeman.
Bradbury, N. A. (2016). Attention span during lectures: 8 seconds, 10 minutes, or more? *Advances in Physiology Education*, 40(4), 509–513.
Day, D. V., Harrison, M. M., & Halpin, S. M. (2008). *An integrative approach to leader development: Connecting adult development, identity, and expertise*. Routledge.
Dehaene, S. (2021). *How we learn: Why brains learn better than any machine... for now*. Penguin.
Dempster, F. N. (1989). Spacing effects and their implications for theory and practice. *Educational Psychology Review*, 1, 309–330.
Elliot, A. J., & Devine, P. G. (1994). On the motivational nature of cognitive dissonance: Dissonance as psychological discomfort. *Journal of Personality and Social Psychology*, 67(3), 382.
Festinger, L. (1957). *A theory of cognitive dissonance*. Row, Peterson.
Flavell, J. H. (1979). Metacognition and cognitive monitoring: A new area of cognitive–developmental inquiry. *American Psychologist*, 34(10), 906.
Holtmaat, A., & Svoboda, K. (2009). Experience-dependent structural synaptic plasticity in the mammalian brain. *Nature Reviews Neuroscience*, 10(9), 647–658.

Karpicke, J. D., & Blunt, J. R. (2011). Retrieval practice produces more learning than elaborative studying with concept mapping. *Science*, 331(6018), 772–775.

Knudsen, E. I. (2007). Fundamental components of attention. *Annual Review of Neuroscience*, 30 (1), 57–78.

Kolb, D. A. (2014). *Experiential learning: Experience as the source of learning and development* (2nd ed.). Pearson.

Livingston, J. A. (2003). Metacognition: An overview. https://eric.ed.gov/?id=ED474273.

Roediger, H. L., & Butler, A. C. (2011). The critical role of retrieval practice in long-term retention. *Trends in Cognitive Sciences*, 15(1), 20–27.

Roediger, H. L., & Karpicke, J. D. (2006). The power of testing memory: Basic research and implications for educational practice. *Perspectives on Psychological Science*, 1(3), 181–210.

Schön, D. A. (1987). *Educating the reflective practitioner: Toward a new design for teaching and learning in the professions.* Jossey-Bass.

7 Learning with Technology and Media

Still within the cognitive dimension of learning, this chapter is dedicated to the principles of learning which relate specifically to multimedia (i.e. audio-visual) sources. That is, this chapter is focused on what research has shown to be the principles at play when learning from a screen—whether it be a mobile device, a computer screen, television, PPT deck, or any other form of technology, media, or some other audio-visual source. The reason for this distinction, and why this merits a dedicated chapter, is because there are very specific adult information processes involved when learning from audio-visual sources.

Multimedia Learning Theory

You may recall from Chapter 4 that our working memory is the phase after sensory information is perceived and processed in the brain, while preexisting schemas from past experiences are rapidly drawn from long-term memory to provide an individual with relevant data and context. Working memory exists to enable a person to make informed decisions while still doing so in a seemingly instantaneous process of see-think-act.

Richard Mayer, a prominent psychology scholar who has focused on learning through multimedia, set forth a learning theory that sought to explain how people process information originating from complex technological sources, such as computer screens, switchboards, televisions, videos, etc., known as the ***multimedia learning theory***. Essentially, any presentation of information that incorporates several sources of relevant output like speech or narration (audio), text, colors, and shapes, that need to be received *simultaneously* to provide someone with a complete understanding falls under the purview of multimedia learning theory (Mayer & Moreno, 1998; Mayer & Anderson, 1991).

Dual Channel Perception

Information first enters our minds through our senses, a phase we explored in Chapter 4 known as *sensory memory*. Humans process incoming sensory information via two channels in particular: (1) auditory and (2) visual (Mayer & Moreno, 1998). Our auditory channel processes sounds, speech, and verbal cues. Our visual channel processes colors, shapes, characters on a page or screen (i.e. letters and words), and movement. In this manner, you might consider the two channels akin to old yellow and red RCA connector cables.

What is important here is that only those items to which we give our attention can be processed by either channel (see Chapter 5). If we do not give adequate attention to an audio and/or visual signal, then that information will simply not remain or persist in our sensory memory. But if we do give sufficient attention to an audio or visual signal, then the information is processed by our sensory memory, which then makes its way to our working memory for further processing.

DOI: 10.4324/9781003593607-9

It is in our working memory that we make conscious sense of the audio (i.e. sounds, speech) and/or visual (i.e. colors, shapes, movement) information we have received. From that point on, the same principles described in Chapter 5 apply regarding the encoding of information into long-term memory.

Limited Capacity

Recall from Chapters 4–5 that our *working memory* is subject to limited capacity. To be more specific, only a limited amount of processing can take place for each of the audio and visual channels at any given time. As stated in Chapter 4, meaningful learning requires that a substantial amount of cognitive processing take place in the audio and visual channels.

Further, recall that a person's attention demands the allocation of cognitive resources. When learning through technology and multimedia, this specifically includes: (A) paying attention to the presented material; (B) mentally organizing the presented material in a coherent structure; and (C) integrating the presented material with existing knowledge. The *increased saliency* phenomenon of attention tells us that our attention is constantly shifting, such that some things become more salient than others at different times (Weinstein et al., 2018). Consider a "Where's Waldo?" puzzle: if the picture is in full color, Waldo is more difficult to spot than if the picture is mostly black and white except for Waldo. Waldo is therefore more *salient* when he is placed against a black and white backdrop.

Cognitive Overload

Regarding cognitive load, Kalyuga stated:

> In order to learn, we need to attend to and process elements of new information, establish key connections between them, integrate them with available knowledge base, and build new or modified knowledge structures. These processes occur in working memory and inevitably impose a cognitive load.
>
> (Kalyuga, 2007, p. 390)

However, when the learner's cognitive processing exceeds the learner's available cognitive capacity, he or she has reached *cognitive overload*. In other words, because each channel has finite capacity for how much information it can process at a given time, cognitive overload refers to the processing demands evoked by the learning task exceeding the processing capacity of the learner's cognitive system.

Mayer et al. (2001) outlined three overarching categories of processing demands on a learner's cognition (Table 7.1). The first is *extraneous processing*, which refers to the processing of information that serves no purpose in achieving an instructional or performance

Table 7.1 Three demands on the learner's cognitive capacity during learning.

Name	*Description*	*Cause*
Extraneous processing	Processing that does not serve the instructional objective	Poor instructional design
Essential processing	Processing aimed at mentally representing the essential presented material	Complexity of the material
Generative processing	Processing aimed at making sense of the material	Motivation to exert effort

Source: Mayer et al. (2001)

objective. The second category of processing is *essential processing*, referring to the initial processing of essential material into mental representations (schema) in the learner's mind. Lastly, *generative processing* is the third category. It refers to any processing that attempts to make sense of material.

Extraneous Processing

Mayer (2021) and Mayer et al. (2001) offered several effects that help further explain the extraneous (i.e. serves no purpose) load on a learner's cognitive system. According to Mayer's *coherence effect*, learners tend to focus only on what is important and fundamental to understand (Mayer et al., 2001). The presence of interesting but otherwise irrelevant information (e.g. fun facts) is actually detrimental to achieving learning outcomes. Worded differently, too much noise detracts from a learner's limited attention and focus. Extending the learning beyond the level of fundamentals can be achieved by providing learners with opportunities to understand the underlying structures and interactions of concepts through reflection and scenario-based or project-based learning. In this way, the learners' focus is on theory during initial instruction, while they develop a deeper, more nuanced understanding through repeated application.

Next, according to Mayer's *redundancy effect*, the presentation of more information does not necessarily equate to more learning (Mayer et al., 2001). In fact, too much information reduces overall learning. Have you ever noticed how quickly you tune-out when a slide deck says the exact same words that the speaker is speaking verbally? Well, you may consider it a cardinal sin to put the *same* information across different channels (text and narration). That is, identical information across different channels just produces more noise—redundant noise, to be exact. The human brain simply loses focus/attention in the presence of redundant noise. So to be crystal clear, our brains experience what is tantamount to "boredom" when seeing the same words on a screen/slide that are being spoken verbally.

At this stage it is worth highlighting this simple fact: not all multimedia messages are created equally—not all are effective. Research has shown that people learn better from the combination of auditory and visual cues that complement one another. Stated differently, people learn better when both words *and* graphics are used in a complimentary fashion, than from words alone (see Mayer & Anderson, 1991). The key principle here is that quality multimedia presentations allow learners to build both verbal and pictorial mental models that can be integrated (which is a core cognitive process required for meaningful learning). Please note: the emphasis here is on *coordination* of images and text, not *duplication*. In this manner, a superior presentation is one in which the verbal narration is building upon and enhancing what is written on a slide.

Mayer (2001) suggested using *signaling* to explicitly point out the most important information to learners. As far as spatial factors are concerned, Mayer also recommended relying on *contiguity* by placing related information in videos and figures near one another. In the case of videos with audio, this mean that related information should be played simultaneously. Additionally, Mayer and Moreno (2003) discovered that mixing up extraneous information from one channel to the other helps to ease the cognitive burden to process information on any one channel—a phenomenon referred to as *off-loading*. In this manner, no one channel is unnecessarily overloaded (Mayer & Moreno, 2003).

Essential Processing

Mayer (2021) offered two specific mechanisms to most efficiently process the essential material: *segmenting* and *pre-training*. To properly segment, Mayer suggested organizing

learning activities and sessions into smaller, more manageable chunks (to thereby maximize a learner's attention). Pre-training includes providing learners with materials or instruction before a learning event that cover any important terminology or nomenclature that is relevant to the learning event.

Generative Processing

To optimize how a learner makes sense of material that he/she is being presented with, Mayer (2021) suggested two additional mechanisms: *personalization* and *generative activities*. For personalization, Mayer recommended presenting information in a conversational tone and make it relatable to the learner's perspective.

To best incorporate generative activities, Mayer suggested providing the learners with opportunities to pause and reflect on what they have learned so far and how the information relates to them, through activities such as short writing assignments.

The cognitive load approach should consider learning and instruction in terms of efficiency instead of effectiveness because the goal of e-learning is to make learning faster and without mental stress. A professional would be wise to perceive the phenomenon of cognitive load in this manner:

> In terms of cognitive cost (cognitive resources spent, mental effort invested, or cognitive load imposed) of achieving instructional effects...In order to learn, we need to attend to and process elements of new information, establish key connections between them, integrate them with available knowledge base, and build new or modified knowledge structures. These processes occur in WM and inevitably impose a cognitive load.
>
> (Kalyuga, 2007, pp. 388, 390)

Essential Cognitive Load

There are two classifications of cognitive load: *essential* and *non-essential*. Essential cognitive load relates to the "essential processing" section above. Essential cognitive load is deemed essential for learning because it helps with comprehending material and constructing new higher-level knowledge. Because this demand on our cognitive processing is essential, it is important that we provide learners with all necessary resources to accommodate such load *without* exceeding the capacity of working memory.

The essential cognitive classification is comprised of two sub-categories: *intrinsic* and *germane*. Intrinsic cognitive load is caused by the complexity of the task or learning material. Complexity can be measured by the amount of interactive learning elements that need to be consider and understood at the same time and by the degree of interactivity between the elements relative to the level of expertise the learner has in that task or domain. Germane cognitive load refers to the load from learning activities that are designed to enhance learner acquisition of specific knowledge schema structures. These include asking learners to explain principles in their own words, or to compare problem-solution procedures between similar contexts.

Non-Essential Cognitive Load

Non-essential cognitive load refers to the diversion of cognitive resources on activities that are irrelevant to the learning, typically the result of poor instructional design. This may

occur for a variety of reasons: separating related elements via space or time like placing info on two separate pages; searching for solutions to a problem without knowledge of a solution procedure; when learners lack the appropriate prior knowledge to apply to the current situation/problem; or when several new elements are introduced at once or are introduced too fast.

E-Learning

Not since the printing press has a technological advancement so greatly impacted how we learn, debate, and disseminate information to each other as the advent of personal computer devices and the proliferation of the internet. Today, each of us has at our fingertips an ocean of information that dwarfs even the ancient library of Alexandria. Of course, not all of that information is well-sourced, and fewer still are presented in a way that effectively facilitates learning. Unsurprisingly, many organizations purposefully seek out trainers, designers, and other learning professionals who are able to navigate the divide and translate evidence-based adult learning principles into powerful and rapidly scalable online training solutions that can be deployed at the click of a computer mouse.

Compared to the other topics discussed so far in this text, e-learning does not possess its own distinct theoretical foundation, per se (Nichols, 2003). Rather, much of the work in the space involves determining best practices and relevant design considerations within a virtual learning environment. As Nichols (2003) explained: "e-learning [is] a means of education as opposed to a mode of education. In other words, e-learning involves the use of several technological tools that can be applied in various contexts; it is not a distinctive educational system in itself" (p. 2).

One advantage of defining e-learning in this way is the flexibility it affords practitioners to apply other theoretical perspectives and modalities *in conjunction with* the unique opportunities that digital learning offers (Nichols, 2003). As a result, understanding the various learning principles being leveraged for e-learning is a useful skill set to possess regardless of a practitioner's preferred approach or job description, since it can be adapted to a variety of different projects and because of the unique benefits it can bring to bear.

E-learning Positives

There are several benefits associated with e-learning. First, consider this very course in which you are participating. A fundamental advantage of an e-learning environment is that it offers a geography-less, boundaryless reach. E-learning allows a person to work from home, collaborate with international colleagues, and simply capitalize on more business opportunities. Second, there is increased flexibility available through e-learning. Organizations have increased opportunity to address learners' needs and/or offer alternative means of instruction through vivid modes such as videos, games, or rich cases/scenarios (Derouin et al., 2005).

Next, e-Learning provides scalability, as organizations can train more people faster and with far less work or manpower. A scaled e-learning solution is often easier to update, design, and distribute with fewer logistical complexities than other more-manual modes (Derouin et al., 2005):

> The key idea to keep in mind is that the true power of educational technology comes not from replicating things that can be done in other ways, but when it is used to do things that couldn't be done without it.
>
> (Thornburg, as cited by Shute & Towle, 2003)

E-learning Negatives

While e-learning affords increased possibilities for learning, there are also increased restrictions as more traditional instructional tools and methods do not always readily apply to a digital learning environment. For example, soft or interpersonal skills are often far more difficult to train in a virtual environment due to the fact they require face-to-face or complicated situational contexts to develop within (Derouin et al., 2005). In addition, learners of any age, may not have access to or be familiar with using a particular device or software. Also, they might possess a medical condition such as dyslexia or color blindness, which interferes with their ability to meaningfully perceive in the visual elements of an online learning experience (e.g. virtual training). Similarly, smaller organizations may lack the funds, hardware, or expertise necessary to effectively deploy e-learning solutions (Sambrook, 2003; Ali & Magalhaes, 2008). And finally, e-learning is typically a self-regulated process, in that learners are often personally responsible for managing their time, pace, and the distractions that will ultimately dictate learning outcomes, as such, when compared to in-person instruction, e-learning demands a greater level of intrinsic motivation and self-discipline from learners in order to be successful (Wong, 2007).

For any learners unequipped to take on this added responsibility, such as failing to employ the learning strategies mentioned in the previous chapter, or when a training program fails to account for the learners' needs in this new learning environment, e-learning solutions may be less effective as a result. Issues like these often become even more pronounced whenever you need to design or facilitate training programs *internationally*, where cultural, linguistic, and socioeconomic factors become more pronounced, and expectations for what e-learning entails tend to differ considerably (Ali & Magalhaes, 2008).

Instructional Videos

For our purposes, I will consider any multimedia instruction in the form of motion picture—whether recorded by camera or from digitally created graphics—plus recorded audio to be an *instructional video* (Mayer & Moreno, 2003; Mayer, 2021). This can be a brief explanatory video, a lecture, a demonstration of how to carry out a task, or an educational show/documentary. Mayer and Moreno (2003) and Mayer (2021) researched the effectiveness of a series of attributes of instructional videos and arrived at several conclusions worth highlighting.

Dynamic Drawing

Mayer and Moreno (2003) and Mayer (2021) found that people learn better from a video lecture when the onscreen instructor draws graphics on a board while lecturing rather than referring to already drawn graphics. That is, a learner achieves greater recall from seeing an instructor draw the text on the board anew, when compared to the presentation of text already drawn.

Gaze Guidance

Learners are sensitive to an instructor's eye gaze. Mayer and Moreno (2003) and Mayer (2021) found that people learn *better* from a video lecture when the onscreen instructor shifts gaze between the audience and board while lecturing rather than looking only at the audience or only at the board. In this manner, writing on a board then looking back at the class is superior to always looking straight at the class, like on a transparent board. The lecturer's occasional shifting of gaze is ideal.

Generative Activity

People learn better from a video lecture when they are asked to engage in summarizing activities during the learning process. According to *generative learning theory*, the act of taking summary notes or physically copying the actions of the instructor in a video can prime three cognitive processes:

1 **Selecting:** which involves focusing on the important information.
2 **Organizing:** which involves building a coherent mental structure.
3 **Integrating:** which involves using relevant prior knowledge.

Therefore, instructional videos should be supplemented with prompts to engage in an appropriate generative (i.e. summarizing or mimicking) activity.

Perspective

People learn better from a video lecture that is filmed from a first-person perspective than a third-person perspective. For "how to" videos, for example, viewing a task from the first-person POV leads to significantly better transfer scores than the same demonstration in third-person.

Subtitle

Mayer and Moreno (2003) and Mayer (2021) found that people learn better from a video documentary or show in the learner's second language when printed subtitles are added or used to replace spoken words. Note: this finding applies to second language viewing only.

Seductive Details

People do not learn better from a multimedia lesson when extraneous video is added. While interesting, learning is not necessarily enhanced by extraneous videos added to a multimedia lesson. Instead, extraneous video can be distracting to the learning experience. Building excitement or arousal in and of itself does not really add value to the learning. So ultimately, the use of videos in the learning process is only effective to the degree to which the video is relevant to the topic. Video for the sake of video is not effective (Mayer & Moreno, 2003; Mayer, 2021).

Application of This Chapter

This chapter is based largely on work of Richard Mayer, whose research is based on cognitive psychology. His work can—and should—be effectively applied by professionals to create more effective learning materials leveraging technology and multimedia. Below I list several specific ways a professional can apply Mayer's principles of multimedia learning:

1 **Multimedia principle:** Consider using both words and visuals rather than just words alone. Incorporate relevant images, graphs, animations, and videos to supplement textual information.
2 **Coherence principle:** Exclude extraneous material that does not contribute to the learning goals. Eliminate unnecessary graphics, sounds, or animations that may cause cognitive overload or distract learners from the main message.

3 **Signaling:** consider highlighting and calling-out key material, both in verbal and visual ways.
4 **Redundancy principle:** Avoid presenting the same information in multiple formats simultaneously. Eliminate redundant information that can cause cognitive overload and interfere with the learning process. In other words, do not write the same thing on the screen that is being said verbally by the speaker. The audio should *compliment* and *supplement* the visual, not repeat the same thing.
5 **Spatial contiguity principle:** Present corresponding words and pictures near each other on the screen. Ensure that text and related graphics are placed physically close to each other on the screen to reduce cognitive load.
6 **Temporal contiguity principle:** Consider presenting corresponding words and pictures simultaneously. Display related information at the same time to facilitate the integration of verbal and visual information.
7 **Segmenting principle:** Break down complex lessons into smaller segments. Present content in manageable chunks, allowing learners to process information more easily and efficiently.
8 **Pre-training principle:** Provide introductory information about key concepts before presenting the main material. This primes learners for upcoming content and aids in better comprehension of the main instructional materials.
9 **Modality principle:** Consider using animation or narration rather than on-screen text. Employing spoken explanations or animations instead of static text can reduce cognitive load, making it easier for learners to grasp complex concepts.
10 **Personalization principle:** Consider using conversational language and personalize the learning experience. Engage learners by addressing them directly and using a friendly tone in the instructional materials.
11 **Voice principle:** Use a friendly, human voice for narration. Choose a voice that is clear, engaging, and easy to understand to enhance the learning experience and maintain learner engagement.

By integrating these principles into the design of learning materials that are audio-visual in nature, professionals can create more effective and engaging learning experiences that promote better understanding, retention, and application of the content by the learners.

References

Ali, G. E., & Magalhaes, R. (2008). Barriers to implementing e-learning: A Kuwaiti case study. *International Journal of Training and Development*, 12(1), 36–53.

Coates, H., James, R., & Baldwin, G. (2005). A critical examination of the effects of learning management systems on university teaching and learning. *Tertiary Education and Management*, 11(1), 19–36.

Derouin, R. E., Fritzsche, B. A., & Salas, E. (2005). E-learning in organizations. *Journal of Management*, 31(6), 920–940.

Kalyuga, S. (2007). Enhancing instructional efficiency of interactive e-learning environments: A cognitive load perspective. *Educational Psychology Review*, 19, 387–399.

Mayer, R. E. (2021). Evidence-based principles for how to design effective instructional videos. *Journal of Applied Research in Memory and Cognition*, 10(2), 229–240.

Mayer, R. E., & Anderson, R. B. (1991). Animations need narrations: An experimental test of a dual-coding hypothesis. *Journal of Educational Psychology*, 83(4), 484.

Mayer, R. E., Heiser, J., & Lonn, S. (2001). Cognitive constraints on multimedia learning: When presenting more material results in less understanding. *Journal of Educational Psychology*, 93(1), 187–198.

Mayer, R. E., & Moreno, R. (1998). A split-attention effect in multimedia learning: Evidence for dual processing systems in working memory. *Journal of Educational Psychology*, 90(2), 312–320.

Mayer, R. E., & Moreno, R. (2003). Nine ways to reduce cognitive load in multimedia learning. *Educational Psychologist*, 38(1), 43–52.

Nichols, M. (2003). A theory for eLearning. *Journal of Educational Technology & Society*, 6(2), 1–10.

Sambrook, S. (2003). E-learning in small organisations. *Education+ Training*, 45(8/9), 506–516.

Shute, V., & Towle, B. (2003). Adaptive e-learning. *Educational Psychologist*, 38(2), 105–114.

Watson, W. R., & Watson, S. L. (2007). An argument for clarity: What are learning management systems, what are they not, and what should they become. *TechTrends*, 51(2), 28–34.

Weinstein, Y., Madan, C. R., & Sumeracki, M. A. (2018). Teaching the science of learning. *Cognitive Research: Principles and Implications*, 3(1), 2.

Wong, D. (2007). A critical literature review on e-learning limitations. *Journal for the Advancement of Science and Arts*, 2(1), 55–62.

Part III

The Behavioral Dimension of Learning

8 Behaviorism and Behavioral Performance

Pavlov, a Dog, and Some Saliva

Perhaps the most famous experiment in history was accidentally stumbled upon. In the 1890s, Russian physiologist Dr. Ivan Pavlov was in the middle of researching the digestive process of dogs. By surgically implanting test tubes into the dogs' cheeks, he was able to measure the saliva while the dogs were being fed. Dr. Pavlov predicted the dogs would salivate when the food was in front of them, but instead he observed that the salivation actually started when the dogs heard the footsteps of his assistant. Based on these observations, Pavlov decided to formally research the mechanisms of the dog's behavior in a more rigorous way.

He then began working with neutral stimuli (i.e. things that did not elicit responses from dogs instinctively) to "condition" the dogs. Specifically, he wanted to extract a response each time a new stimulus was introduced. To accomplish this, he used a metronome and turned it on right before giving the dogs food. Over time, the sounds of the clicking metronome caused the dogs to salivate.

- **Unconditioned stimulus** (food) → **Unconditioned response** (salivate)
- **Conditioned stimulus** (metronome sound) → **Conditioned response** (salivate)

Pavlov's discovery is what we now refer to as *classical conditioning*. In this case, the dogs learned to associate an unconditioned stimulus (i.e. food) that already elicited a particular response (i.e. salivating) with a new conditioned stimulus (i.e. metronome), so that the new stimulus brought about the same response. Meaning, when the metronome sounded, the dog would salivate, even without the food being present. For our purposes, the importance of Pavlov's classical conditioning discovery rests in how it led directly to the theory of behaviorism.

Behaviorism

Behaviorism took root in the early 1900s with the work of Dr. John Watson, who studied the behavior of children, and then later Dr. B. F. Skinner—who studied operant conditioning. There was a time when behaviorism was the prevailing theory of learning thanks largely to it being one of the first attempts to study human behavior in a scientifically valid way, making its discoveries not only insightful but replicable. Without question, if this textbook was written 60–70 years ago, behaviorism would be the theory that had the most research behind it, and would occupy many of the pages therein. In fact, in 1928 Dr. Edward Thorndike wrote the first book on learning, titled *Adult Learning*, which was

DOI: 10.4324/9781003593607-11

largely based on the principles of behaviorism. For much of the next 25–35 years behaviorism would be the prevailing learning theory, until the focus shifted to more cognitive theories.

According to the theory of ***behaviorism***, learning is the result of an environmental stimulus influencing how a person thinks and behaves. More specifically, operant conditioning refers to the process where behavior is positively rewarded will likely continue and is, therefore, "learned," while behavior that is negatively reinforced or punished will likely cease to continue (extinction) and is, therefore, "not learned." The key marker of learning based on the theory of behaviorism is a person's change in *observable* behavior—that is, behavior that can be identified, repeated, and measured.

Today, we see elements of behaviorism implanted all around us. For example, a parent might *reinforce* a child's behavior with a compliment or *punish* them for doing something they want to stop. A man might *reward* himself with a gift for achieving a fitness goal. A teenager might see the improvements in ball flight from changes made to his golf swing, and therefore continue the new hand-eye path. Or an employee may put in extra hours on a project in order to avoid being reprimanded (negative reinforcement).

Behaviorism is also seen all over K-12 education and in adult settings. An instructional designer (ID) or learning experience designer (LXD) will use *performance objectives*—which are highly behavioral in nature—to characterize (1) what the learner is expected to be able to do or produce (behavior), (2) the conditions under which the performance is expected to occur (reinforcement), and (3) the level of competence that should be achieved in doing the performance (competence). Further, much of career and vocational education across industries is centered on developing job-related skills.

Learning Behavioral Performances

Recall that the "S" in KSA stands for *skills*, which for our purposes is synonymous with *behaviors* as well as any *physical* or *motor performance*. We now shift our focus to the nature of learning to successfully perform behaviors, skills, and physical movements of the body. In considering the Top Gun example, we know that the program succeeded because it emphasized *doing*. The significance is found in what the trainee pilots were able to *do* under duress.

The key question for us becomes "How do we improve behaviors, skills, and physical performances?" This is different from "How do we teach the relevant knowledge?" For our interests, the key is to set up conditions under which individuals can develop behaviors/skills (i.e. apply what they have learned; or "transfer" their training). The steps toward more effective development of behaviors/skills include: (1) determine with some certainty who the experts are (i.e. people who consistently perform more effectively than their peers); then (2) determine what underlies that superior, more effective performance. And how do we determine what underlies a superior performance? There are a number of ways. For example, we might seek retrospective reports, or we might observe real-time a top performer in action, or which tasks are easier or harder for a non-top performer. We might conduct a think-aloud exercise, where we present a top performer with a situation and ask him or her to vocalize the thought process (i.e. their intuition) behind how they conceptualize the problem and then go about resolving it. Realistically, one might consider a combination of these ideas.

If a person's mind is wandering or too relaxed and just having fun, they probably will not improve. As we discussed in Chapter 5, focused attention is essential; whatever a person is doing should receive one's focus. For example, the key to excellence in swimming lay in maintaining close attention to every detail of performance. You want each stroke done

correctly, time and again, until excellence in every detail becomes a firmly ingrained habit. For this reason, shorter training sessions with clearer goals are the best way to develop new skills faster. In fact, psychological research shows that due to our finite capacity to maintain attention—a phenomenon referred to as "attention economy" (Davenport & Beck, 2001)—it is more effective to train for 100% effort over less time, than at 70% effort for a longer period (Lindsay, 2020; Samuels & Szabadi, 2008). The Yerkes–Dodson law describes the nonlinear relationship between arousal and performance on challenging tasks (Yerkes & Dodson, 1908). Specifically, the research of Yerkes and Dodson found that too much mental arousal for too long of time is counterproductive to eliciting top performance.

In medicine, knowing what the best surgeons do right, and knowing the most common mistakes, make it possible to design an effective surgical training exercise outside the operating room to improve surgeons' mental models. One way would be to use videos of actual surgeries, run them up to a certain decision point, then stop them and ask, "What do you do next?" or "What are you looking at here?" Doctors could run hundreds of these practices until they develop effective mental models. This approach could be applied to a variety of areas where someone could practice something repeatedly "offline" (away from real job where mistakes have real consequences). To improve simulator training, individuals responsible for medical training should determine which errors are most common and most dangerous and focus on those.

In the attempt to learn, grow, and improve our performance of behaviors/skills, we should not dismiss the benefit of manufacturing our own opportunities. As we learned in Chapter 2, having a teacher/coach is ideal because they provide feedback. But make no mistake, not having a teacher/coach works too. Any person can break a skill down into component parts that can be done repeatedly and analyze effectively, determine your weaknesses, and figure out ways to address them. Stated simply, you should pay attention to what you got wrong, and make the necessary corrections. For example, in chess a person might study the games of the grandmasters, trying to reproduce them move by move. Then should he/she choose a move that is different from what the grandmaster chose, they would do well to study the position again to see what was missed.

Behaviors Still Have A Cognitive Element

Combining the ideas discussed in this chapter, it is critical to highlight that expert behavior still has a cognitive component to it. Worded differently, skill acquisition is both physical and mental. This takes us back to Chapter 2 and the discussion of mental models.

Regardless of the access to a teacher/coach, a person can only form the effective mental representations necessary for a top performance when they attempt to reproduce what the expert performer does, fails, determines why the failure occurred, and tries again…and repeats. Successful mental models are inextricably tied to behaviors/skills/actions, and it is the effort to reproduce the original product (i.e. through practice) that will yield the mental representations we seek. To accomplish this, we might ask a top performer to describe what they are *thinking* as they perform a task (i.e. think-alouds).

To be completely clear, a key ability of expert/top performers is the ability to recognize unexpected situations, quickly consider various possible responses, and decide on the best one. For example, research on top surgeons shows that while they have prepared surgical plans before they start, they regularly monitor the surgery-in-progress and are ready to switch gears if necessary. Top surgeons have a mental representation of how it should go, they visualize, and are constantly comparing the visual against the actual surgery so they can detect when something is wrong and adapt accordingly.

A standard approach for examining mental representations that people use to guide themselves through a task is to stop them in the middle of the task, turn out the lights, and ask them to describe the current situation, what has happened, and what is about to happen. It is ideal to further combine interviews *and* observations when trying to understand the mental representations of experts.

Role of Mistakes and Errors

As we discussed in Chapter 2, learners can leverage errors to optimize the learning of a behavior/skill. Errors cue the nervous system for neuroplasticity (think: "errors open the door"). That is, the recognition of mistakes/errors tells the nervous system that something needs to change (Norman et al., 2021). For example, if you are learning a new skill, errors tell the brain to be open to plasticity. Specifically, errors cue (1) the frontal cortex and the (2) neuromodulators (norepinephrine, acetylcholine, dopamine) that allow for plasticity.

When trying to learn a new skill, it is helpful to think: "The more mistakes you make, the more plastic your brain becomes." This is true to the degree that when you do get a skill right, that correct pattern will be rewarded and consolidated. Without errors, the brain is simply not in a strong position to change itself.

Transfer of Training

The *transfer of training* refers to "The extent to which the learning that results from a training experience transfers to the job and leads to meaningful changes in work performance" (Ford et al., 2018, p. 202). Blume et al. (2010) conducted a meta-analysis of 89 studies and identified three conditions that help enhance the successful transfer and application of training: *work climate* had the highest relationship with transfer, the next was *support*, and third was *work constraints*. Schindler and Burkholder (2016) defined *support* as a multidimensional construct that includes elements from mentoring, coaching, social support, and task support.

Additionally, Hageman (1983) reviewed 13 studies conducted on military retention of psychomotor tasks. They found that memory retention was enhanced by:

- increasing the amount of task repetitions;
- testing during training;
- spaced practice; and
- a variety of equipment worked on during training;

They also found that *cognitive ability* predicted the proficiency level at the acquisition/learning stage, but the rate of forgetting over time was similar for individuals with high and low cognitive ability.

The noteworthy part of this 1983 research is how much it overlaps with the concepts from general expertise development covered in Chapter 2.

Application of This Chapter

Behaviorism is a learning theory that emphasizes observable behaviors and external stimuli as the primary factors influencing learning. While modern instructional design often incorporates a variety of learning theories, behaviorism can still inform the design of effective learning experiences. Here are several ways in which professionals can apply the principles of behaviorism:

- **Clearly defined objectives:** Set clear and measurable learning objectives. Behaviorism emphasizes observable behaviors, so objectives should specify what learners will be able to do or demonstrate after completing the instruction.
- **Structured learning:** Break down complex tasks into smaller, more manageable steps. Behaviorism supports the idea that learning is an accumulation of small, observable behaviors. Design instructional sequences that guide learners through a step-by-step process.
- **Reinforcement:** Provide reinforcement for correct responses or behaviors. Positive reinforcement can include praise, rewards, or acknowledgment, while negative reinforcement involves removing undesirable elements. Feedback should be immediate and linked to specific behaviors.
- **Practice and repetition:** Include opportunities for learners to practice and repeat tasks. Behaviorism suggests that repeated practice strengthens the association between stimuli and responses, leading to more automatic and enduring learning.
- **Use of models:** Present learners with models or examples of desired behaviors. Observing others can serve as a powerful form of learning, as suggested by behaviorism. This can be achieved through case studies, demonstrations, or simulations.
- **Scaffolding:** Provide support and guidance as learners progress. Gradually reduce support as learners become more competent. This process, known as scaffolding, aligns with behaviorist principles by helping learners build on existing knowledge and skills.
- **Immediate feedback:** Offer immediate feedback on learner performance. Timely feedback reinforces correct responses and helps learners adjust their behavior for improvement. The immediacy of feedback is a key aspect of behaviorist instructional strategies.
- **Use of stimulus–response associations:** Design activities that strengthen the association between stimuli and responses. This could involve scenario-based learning where learners must respond to specific situations with the correct behavior.
- **Clear instruction and expectations:** Clearly communicate instructions and expectations. Clarity in communication is essential in behaviorist approaches to ensure that learners understand what is expected of them and what the consequences of their actions will be.
- **Assessment of learning outcomes:** Design assessments that measure observable behaviors related to the learning objectives. Behaviorist assessments often focus on what learners can demonstrate or perform rather than solely on their declarative knowledge.

Merriam and Bierema (2014) made the following observation: "As reflective practitioners, it is important to recognize the role of feedback, the nature of reinforcement, learning objectives, and behavior modification in structuring learning activities for adults" (p. 28). While behaviorism is just one of many learning theories, incorporating these principles can contribute to the creation of effective learning designs, especially in contexts where observable behaviors and outcomes are critical.

References

Blume, B. D., Ford, J. K., Baldwin, T. T., & Huang, J. L. (2010). Transfer of training: A meta-analytic review. *Journal of Management*, 36(4), 1065–1105.

Davenport, T. H., & Beck, J. C. (2001). The attention economy. *Ubiquity*, 2001 (May), 1.

Ford, J. K., Baldwin, T. T., & Prasad, J. (2018). Transfer of training: The known and the unknown. *Annual Review of Organizational Psychology and Organizational Behavior*, 5, 201–225.

Hageman, D. (1983). Effectiveness of two-dimensional simulation in avionics procedural training. https://arc.aiaa.org/doi/abs/10.2514/6.1984-516.

Lindsay, G. W. (2020). Attention in psychology, neuroscience, and machine learning. *Frontiers in Computational Neuroscience*, 14, 29.

Merriam, S. B., & Bierema, L. L. (2014). *Adult learning: Linking theory and practice*. John Wiley & Sons.

Norman, K. J., Riceberg, J. S., Koike, H., Bateh, J., McCraney, S. E., Caro, K., ... & Morishita, H. (2021). Post-error recruitment of frontal sensory cortical projections promotes attention in mice. *Neuron*, 109(7), 1202–1213.

Samuels, E. R., & Szabadi, E. (2008). Functional neuroanatomy of the noradrenergic locus coeruleus: Its roles in the regulation of arousal and autonomic function. *Current Neuropharmacology*, 6 (3), 235–253.

Schindler, L. A., & Burkholder, G. J. (2016). A mixed methods examination of the influence of dimensions of support on training transfer. *Journal of Mixed Methods Research*, 10(3), 292–310.

Yerkes, R. M., & Dodson, J. D. (1908). The relation of strength of stimulus to rapidity of habit-formation. In E. E. Boe & R. M. Church (Eds.), *Punishment: Issues and experiments*, 27–41. Appleton-Century-Crofts.

9 Motivation

The Stanford Marshmallow Experiment

While some research experiments are famous because of the knowledge they produce for the scientific world, others are equally as famous for the controversy surrounding the methods used by the researchers or the results themselves (see the Milgram experiments, the Little Albert experiment, the Stanford Prison experiment, or the Harvard Human experiments). One other famous example of controversy meeting deep insight is the *Stanford Marshmallow Experiment.*

In 1972, a Stanford University research team, led by psychology professor Walter Mischel, sought to explore the phenomenon of delayed gratification. To accomplish this, the team invited 50 children—25 boys, 25 girls—from ages 3 to 5 years old, to enter a room, one at a time. In front of each child, on the table, was placed a toy along with a tin that

Figure 9.1 The Stanford Marshmallow Experiment
Source: Photo by FlyD on Unsplash

DOI: 10.4324/9781003593607-12

contained a small marshmallow. The researcher told each child to play with the toy as he left the room, and that if the child did not eat the marshmallow while he was away then he would reward them with a second marshmallow upon his return. However, if the child decided to eat the first one before the researcher came back, then they would not get a second marshmallow. Essentially the choice became one treat now versus two treats later. The researcher then left the room for approximately 15 minutes.

As you can imagine, the grainy video footage of the children waiting alone in the room was entertaining. Some kids immediately jumped up and ate the first marshmallow as soon as the researcher closed the door. Others, wrestled with making a choice, wiggled and scooted in their chairs as they tried to show restraint, but eventually gave in to temptation a few minutes later. A few children did manage to wait the entire time. However, the fascinating part came years later.

The researchers continued to follow each child for more than 40 years. The children who waited to receive the second marshmallow ended up having higher SAT scores, lower levels of substance abuse, lower likelihood of obesity, better responses to stress, better social skills (as reported by their parents), and generally better scores in a range of other life measures. Repeatedly and consistently, the group who waited patiently for the second marshmallow succeeded in whatever capacity the researchers measured. In other words, this series of experiments proved that the ability to delay gratification was critical for success in life.

Yet with all the studies surrounding the Marshmallow experiment, the researchers never firmly understood the motivations behind each child's initial choice to eat the first marshmallow or wait for a second one. So, after all these years the lack of understanding invites the fundamental question, "Why do people do what they do?"

Defining Motivation

I agree wholeheartedly with Wlodkowski and Ginsberg (2008), who stated, "If something can be learned, it can be learned in a motivating manner ... every instructional plan also needs to be a motivational plan" (pp. 46–47). This statement encompasses everything I believe about the professional's responsibility: that every ID/LXD initiative should simultaneously consider and incorporate a motivational plan. Worded differently, I believe it is irresponsible for a practitioner to ignore the motivational quality of the instruction or learning experience one is designing. To effectively do so, it is necessary to understand what drives adult motivation.

Pintrich argued that to truly understand the construct of motivation, it should be explored from multiple angles and informed by multiple disciplines. He stated:

> Just as cognitive, developmental, and the learning sciences draw from psychology, anthropology, sociology, linguistics, philosophy, artificial intelligence, neuroscience, biology, and education, motivational sciences could draw from multiple disciplinary perspectives in terms of theories, constructs, and methods to address questions regarding the role of student motivation. The diversity of disciplinary approaches should lead to the evolution of motivational science as different ideas and constructs have different levels of relative success in helping us understand motivational phenomena.
>
> (Pintrich, 2003, p. 668)

Therefore, to be clear, *motivation* is a broad construct. That is, there are multiple theories of motivation and sub-theories within those. Individuals can have a high level of motivation for one activity and very low motivation for another. For example, you may have very high motivation to learn in a particular course but have low motivation to exercise. Motivation

can also change with time, including within a single day. In short, the topic of motivation is dynamic and expansive. In the broadest sense, however, ***motivation*** is the energy we put into accomplishing something. There are many psychological and social factors at work for and against a person exerting such energy and taking said action.

In learning and development, you will often see discussions of ***extrinsic*** and ***intrinsic*** motivation. ***Extrinsic motivation*** relates to sources of motivation that come external to the individual. Extrinsic motivation typically pertains to rewards (e.g. a carrot) such as money, prizes, points, etc. given to an individual to induce performance, or deterrents (e.g. a stick) such as penalties, fines, or criticism. ***Intrinsic motivation***, conversely, is found within a person; it is the desire to perform well because it satisfies an individual's basic psychological needs to feel competent, to belong, and to have a sense of control over self (Ryan & Deci, 2017). Which do you think is a more powerful, long-term motivator: extrinsic or intrinsic motivation? Fortunately, the research is clear: an individual's intrinsic motivation from within that is most powerful and most enduring (Kulkarni, 2015). Fortunately, we know through research that much can be done to create support for people to experience greater intrinsic motivation.

Theories of Motivation

I focus on three leading theories of learning: a cognitive view, a need-driven perspective, and self-determination theory.

A Cognitive View of Motivation

A cognitive view of motivation emphasizes the role of mental processes—such as beliefs, expectations, goals, and attributions—in driving human behavior. Rather than being primarily influenced by external rewards or internal drives, a cognitive view focuses on how *people think* about their actions, the meaning they assign to outcomes, and how they mentally process experiences to determine their motivation. Clark (2008) argued that cognitive views of motivation put the individual's beliefs at the center. These are important when individuals have a choice to select a learning goal or event.

Need-Driven Motivation

Abraham Maslow's (1943) famous hierarchy of needs is a humanistic theory of motivation that posits behavior can be envisioned as a series of stages involving an increasing list of needs. The key takeaway being that before someone can move on to the next stage, *they must first satisfy all the needs in the preceding stage.* For example, someone who is starving is not going to be concerned with finding love so much as finding something to eat.

As such, the hierarchy naturally starts with basic physiological concerns including, the need for food, water, shelter, and safety, before expanding to encompass less immediate environmental concerns such as property and resources. As those more pressing needs are satisfied, individuals can turn their focus inward and begin to work towards their intrinsic motivations, such as finding love, friendship, and a sense of purpose and place in the world. If a person is fortunate enough to meet all their needs, they reach the point referred to as *self-actualization*, where the result is the ability to realize their full and truest potential in the world.

Self-determination Theory

Ryan and Deci (2000, 2017) synthesized a great deal of research that each of the authors had conducted over many years to explain different types of motivation (i.e. amotivation,

extrinsic motivation, and intrinsic motivation). In short, they concluded that individuals become "self-determined" to the degree to which their needs for (1) competence, (2) connection, and (3) autonomy are fulfilled. The term *self-determination* essentially refers to an individual's internal level of determination (i.e. their motivation). According to Ryan and Deci (2000), the presence of the triad of *competence, connection*, and *autonomy* create the optimal conditions to produce the highest degree of intrinsic motivation. (Note: in the scholarly literature, "volition" is a synonymous term to intrinsic motivation.) These needs have consistently shown to be essential for motivation and well-being across various contexts. He states these needs emerged empirically from research showing their role in facilitating intrinsic motivation and internalization of values.

Ryan and Deci (2000) connected differing motivational states to behaviors that ranged from *non-self-determined* to *self-determined* with the important finding that people who act with greater self-determination experience far more positive outcomes than those who are non-self-determined. Self-determination theory helps connect the source of the regulation, or "perceived forces that move a person to act," (Ryan & Deci, 2000, p. 69) to the kind of motivation demonstrated.

Research has found that higher states of *autonomy* on the motivation continuum correlates with better outcomes in well-being, performance, and congruence. When the source of regulation is internal that may be associated with an integrated regulatory style. The person sees the desired action as congruent with their needs or values, so even though there may be elements of extrinsic motivation (e.g. grades in a course for their graduate program). Extending the example further, the motivation to earn an A in a course is not considered intrinsic motivation, according to self-determination theory, because the outcome (a grade, an earned degree) is not fully driven by the individual.

Motivation in Adult Learning

Houle's (1961) salient work identified three types of motivations for learners: goal-oriented, activity-oriented, and learning-oriented. *Goal-oriented learners* exert effort to learn so that they may attain another goal. In this way, learning is an intermediate step enroute to a larger objective. This type of learning is most typically extrinsic in nature. For example, a person might choose to attend a training program solely to qualify for a promotion. *Activity-oriented learners* engage in a learning experience for the sociality of the event. This type of learning is motivated by one's intrinsic social needs. For instance, a person signs-up for a community class to interact with others and meet new friends. Third, *learning-oriented learners* are interested in learning for the sake of genuine learning. This type of learning is also intrinsically motivated. A person might pursue a certain topic (e.g. World War 1 history) based on love for that topic, with no other ulterior motive or purpose.

Keller's ARCS

Keller (1983) highlighted four conditions of motivation with respect to learning, whose acronym forms *ARCS*: **a**ttention, **r**elevance, **c**onfidence, and **s**atisfaction. As we know from Chapter 5, *attention* is a prerequisite for learning. To be completely clear, the goal for professionals is to capture and sustain the learner's attention. Keller (1983) argued, "A real challenge is to sustain it, to produce a satisfactory level of attention throughout a period of instruction" (p. 3). *Relevance* is an important condition because it essentially answers the questions of "*why*." Relevance can be established explicitly in the content itself, or it can stem from the manner in which something is taught. A learner will perceive relevance to the degree that a learning experience provides opportunities for the learner to satisfy their

various needs. *Confidence* pertains to the learner's expectancy for success. The key to this condition is to deploy strategies aimed at helping the learner believe that some level of success is achievable with a level of effort exerted. Lastly, the fourth condition refers to the feeling of *satisfaction* for what is being learned. Research shows that people feel greater motivation when objectives, tasks, and activities are clearly defined (Sullivan & Strode, 2010; Barron & Harackiewicz, 2000). Individuals also experience greater motivation when rewards and reinforcement are used that align with the objectives, tasks, and activities. People also experience increased satisfaction when the feedback they receive is clear and the path toward improvement contains sufficient detail and help (Tricomi & DePasque, 2016).

Motivation When Learning Online

The research is clear: "online learning presents many challenges in terms of keeping students motivated to pursue their goals" (Esra & Sevilen, 2021, p. 20). Hartnett (2011) researched learner motivation in online environments and concluded that *relevance* was a critical feature of motivation content. Then in a follow-up study one decade later, learners "reported higher levels of engagement when they found the activities and classes relevant to their targets and when they acknowledged that the tasks were meaningful for them" (Esra & Sevilen, 2021, p. 20).

Lin et al. (2017) concluded that despite a variety of factors, the influence of a teacher, facilitator, or trainer proved to be the key moderating variable. Lin et al. (2017) observed, "The key in developing the effectiveness of digital learning on teaching lies in teachers" (p. 3554). That is, any difficulties or challenges with learner motivation stemming from the online environment itself could (or, rather, should) be overcome by the practices and efficacy of the teacher/facilitator/trainer. Of note, Ushida (2005) and Chen and Jang (2010) found that *detailed feedback* heightened the motivation for online learners. And lastly, Özhan and Kocadere (2020) and Esra and Sevilen (2021) found that *gamified content* served as a motivation booster as well.

Application Of This Chapter

An adult's motivation to learn is impacted by several variables. Therefore, it is wise to assume a holistic, 360-degree view, while considering as many angles as possible. Remember, "If something can be learned, it can be learned in a motivating manner ... every instructional plan also needs to be a motivational plan" (Wlodkowski & Ginsberg, 2008, pp. 46–47). I repeat this quote because I find Wlodkowski and Ginsberg's statement to be highly relevant for a chapter on motivation such as this. We may ask, "What is the manner in which to best apply the principles of motivation?"

First, when designing learning experiences, practitioners should (1) *know* and (2) *consider* the needs and attributes of the learners. Smart practice would then compare the learners' needs and attributes against the principles of motivation. Second, practitioners should balance the *many* with the *few*. That is, there will often be patterns of needs and attributes from most learners; there will also be needs and attributes unique to a small few (consider the principles discussed in Chapter 3, for example). The savvy practitioner will consider both the *many* and the *few* simultaneously and find a way to account for each. To accomplish this, professionals should consider the following key questions:

- What are the learning needs of our learners? What are their key attributes?
- What do many/most learners need? What are, if any, the unique needs/attributes?
- How do their learning needs and attributes marry with the motivation principles discussed in this chapter?

References

Barron, K. E., & Harackiewicz, J. M. (2000). Achievement goals and optimal motivation: A multiple goals approach. In *Intrinsic and extrinsic motivation* (pp. 229–254). Academic Press.

Chen, K. C. & Jang, S. J. (2010). Motivation in online learning: Testing a model of self-determination theory. *Computers in Human Behavior*, 26(4), 741–752.

Clark, R. C. (2008). *Building expertise: Cognitive methods for training and performance improvement.* John Wiley & Sons.

Esra, M. E. Ş. E., & Sevilen, Ç. (2021). Factors influencing EFL students' motivation in online learning: A qualitative case study. *Journal of Educational Technology and Online Learning*, 4(1), 11–22.

Hartnett, M. (2011). Examining motivation in online distance learning environments: Complex, multifaceted, and situation-dependent. *International Review of Resarch in Open and Distributed Learning*, 12(6), 20–38.

Houle, C. O. (1961). *The inquiring mind.* University of Wisconsin Press.

Keller, J. M. (1983). Motivational design of instruction. In C. M. Reigeluth (Eds.), *Instructional design theories and models: An overview of their current status* (pp. 383–434). Routledge.

Kulkarni, S. M. (2015). A review on intrinsic motivation: A key to sustainable and effective leadership. *Review of Integrative Business and Economics Research*, 4(3), 74.

Lin, M. H., Chen, H. C., & Liu, K. S. (2017). A study of the effects of digital learning on learning motivation and learning outcome. *Eurasia Journal of Mathematics, Science and Technology Education*, 13(7), 3553–3564.

Maslow, A. H. (1943). A theory of human motivation. *Psychological Review*, 50(4), 370–396.

Özhan, Ş. Ç., & Kocadere, S. A. (2020). The effects of flow, emotional engagement, and motivation on success in a gamified online learning environment. *Journal of Educational Computing Research*, 57(8), 2006–2031.

Pintrich, P. R. (2003). A motivational science perspective on the role of student motivation in learning and teaching contexts. *Journal of Educational Psychology*, 95(4), 667.

Ryan, R. M., & Deci, E. L. (2000). Self-determination theory and the facilitation of intrinsic motivation, social development, and well-being. *American Psychologist*, 55(1), 68–78.

Ryan, R. M., & Deci, E. L. (2017). *Self-determination theory: Basic psychological needs in motivation, development, and wellness.* Guilford Press.

Sullivan, G. S., & Strode, J. P. (2010). Motivation through goal setting: A self-determined perspective. *Strategies*, 23(6), 19.

Tricomi, E., & DePasque, S. (2016). The role of feedback in learning and motivation. In *Recent developments in neuroscience research on human motivation* (Vol. 19, pp. 175–202). Emerald.

Ushida, E. (2005). The role of students' attitudes and motivation in second language learning in online language courses. *CALICO Journal*, 23(1), 49–78.

Wlodkowski, R. J., & Ginsberg, M. B. (2017). *Enhancing adult motivation to learn: A comprehensive guide for teaching all adults.* John Wiley & Sons.

Part IV

The Socio-Emotional Dimension of Learning

10 Social Constructivism and Social Learning Theory

The first two dimensions of learning discussed thus far—the cognitive (Part II) and the behavioral (Part III)—were clearly and singularly delineated. But while we discuss the three learning dimensions separately, they each impact the other two. And to be clear, this third dimension of learning, the socio-emotional dimension (Part IV), is one that *significantly* impacts a person's cognitive and behavioral dimensions of learning. In fact, a key tenet of the socio-emotional dimension is that research has found that a lack of socio-emotional skills can altogether thwart an individual's expertise development, even if they possess otherwise high potential (Subotnik & Jarvin, 2005). So, because the goal is to maximize our expertise development, as well as that of others, it is essential to understand how to develop our socio-emotional skills in the most optimal way possible.

"Sense-making posits the human experience as, in part, an active, *socially rooted* process of creating sense or meaning out of information problems, discontinuities, and disconnections, all of which are encountered in our personal and professional lives" (Westbrook, 2006, emphasis added). To introduce the socio-emotional dimension of learning, in this chapter I will begin by discussing social constructivism and social learning theory. The foundation of social constructivism dates back to the early twentieth-century Soviet Union with the work of psychologist Lev Vygotsky. During his lifetime, Vygotsky's work focused largely on cognitive development and mental functioning. However, in the nearly one hundred years since his passing, many of his ideas still successfully inform our understanding of adult learning.

Constructivism

However, before discussing social constructivism, it is necessary to first define constructivism. Constructivism is a learning theory that suggests learners actively "construct" their own understanding of the world and knowledge through their experiences and interactions (Amineh & Asl, 2015). It contrasts with historically older views of learning that portray learners as passive recipients of information. In constructivism, learners are seen as individuals who build knowledge by connecting new information to their existing mental frameworks and experiences. The key principles of constructivism include active learning, prior knowledge, scaffolding, reflection, authentic tasks, and critical thinking. Historically, constructivism has had a significant impact on learning practices, influencing curriculum design, instructional strategies, and assessment methods. It aligns well with student-centered and inquiry-based learning approaches, emphasizing the importance of engaging learners in meaningful, authentic tasks that promote deep understanding and transferable skills.

Internalization

To understand how Vygotsky envisioned learning and how it functioned, we begin with his concept of *internalization*. Stated simply, you can consider the principle of internalization

DOI: 10.4324/9781003593607-14

Table 10.1 Internalization of various physical or socio-cultural constructs.

Construct type	*Mental model example*
Meanings	Hammer and sickle
Signs	Military salute; clapping (to cheer)
Symbols	Nike swoosh; Apple logo
Concepts	Good vs. evil

to be the practice of observation and imitation. According to Vygotsky's view of internalization, an individual can observe and "internalize" the world around them as they engage in social interaction. It is during social interaction that an individual's thinking is transformed.

Extending this idea further, internalization represents the physical and socio-cultural constructs (ideas) that we experience from interacting with the external world. These constructs include physical and sociocultural meanings, signs, symbols, and concepts which we transform into mental models/representations/schema in the mind of the learner to be utilized in future efforts to make sense of the world around them.

To use his own words, this is how Vygotsky (1978) himself explained the internalization process:

(A) An operation initially represents an external activity is reconstructed and begins to occur internally.
(B) An *inter*personal process is transformed into an *intra*personal one.
(C) The transformation of an interpersonal process into an intrapersonal one is the result of a long series of developmental events.

(Vygotsky, 1978, pp. 57–58, emphasis added)

Social Constructivism

Vygotsky's early notion of internalization eventually gave rise to the theory of social constructivism, which shares several similarities with how cognitivism describes learning. Specifically, social constructivism maintains that learning is an internal process within the mind that involves the construction of mental representations from personal experiences (recall Chapters 2 and 4). This is not merely a coincidence because with Vygotsky the intuition behind social constructivism drew heavily from the early writings of cognitivist thinkers during its initial conception.

Where cognitivism and social constructivism diverge most is in how knowledge encoding occurs in the mind. Under *social constructivism*, learning is foremost a social process wherein an individual's knowledge is connected to whatever sociocultural environment they find themselves a part of. Consider how you learned the nuances of language, was it based on the environment in which you were raised, or was it through "study?" In this way, knowledge becomes less of a static construct occupying space in any one person's mind and instead becomes something more fluid: a river of information that ebbs and flows rapidly in response to shifting environmental stimuli and pressures. Much like any river, your mind is bound to be influenced not by personal decisions so much as by outside forces influencing your perceptions and judgments.

Now consider for a moment everything you have learned up to this point. Without question this is not an easy task, but now I want you to estimate how much of that

knowledge was a result of only the things you figured out entirely on your own. For most of us, the majority of the knowledge we possess is a culmination of being taught, mentored, and through gradual observation of a more-knowledgeable individual, whether by a sibling, parent, professor, or coach.

To be clear, constructivism and social constructivism are *very* closely related. Both constructivism and social constructivism are grounded in the idea that learners actively "construct" knowledge and meaning from their experiences, rather than passively receiving information from the external world. The emphasis for both is on the role of the learner (i.e. the person doing the "constructing") in the learning process. Where they differ, naturally, is the emphasis placed on social interaction.

Zone of Proximal Development

Building on the concept of internalization, let us next discuss the *zone of proximal development* (ZPD). Vygotsky's ZPD refers to the range (or "zone") of tasks or activities that a learner cannot perform independently, but *can* accomplish with the guidance and support of a more knowledgeable person, typically a teacher, mentor, or peer (Vygotsky, 1978).

To illustrate, let us consider the example of learning to ride a bike. Whenever someone first attempts to ride a bike, mentors provide training support or instructional scaffolding that enable learners to perform the action before they are capable of doing it independently. In the case of riding a bike, one starts by providing a novice with training wheels and some basic instruction as scaffolds to kickstart the learning process. Of course, given enough time and practice, the learners' capabilities start to outpace the support necessary as their zone of proximal development, or level of expertise, continues to rise. For the learner to develop the more complex skills related to the task, mentors gradually remove those initial scaffolds, meaning the training wheels come off and the learner takes on the greater challenge of relying more on their own knowledge and skills (KSAs) to perform the task successfully. By keeping the focus on skills *slightly* outside of the learner's zone of proximal development, the learning process never becomes stagnant, boring, or overwhelming for our learners.

Social Learning Theory

A sibling theory that shares many similarities with the tenets of social constructivism is *social learning theory*, which comes to us from Dr. Albert Bandura. Dr. Bandura sought to build a more comprehensive understanding of how humans learn by considering how social factors and the environment influence learning and behavior. Dr. Bandura sought to borrow many tenets of behaviorism such as operant conditioning, where rewards and punishments serve as the principal drivers of behavioral change. As a result, Bandura's experiments primarily centered around the role of observational learning, that is, how various KSAs can be acquired or extinguished by witnessing someone else completing an action and subsequently being rewarded or punished for their behavior.

In his most famous experiments (Bandura et al., 1961), one of Bandura's assistants would sit in a room with a young volunteer only a few years old. Depending on test conditions the child would witness the assistant accosting a blow-up Bobo doll with their hands and various toy implements.

Alternatively, in other cases, the assistant merely ignored the doll, opting instead to play with the other toys in the room. Afterward, the assistant was either rewarded or punished by another lab member. Once the volunteers witnessed this outcome, they were then placed alone in another play area with the same instruments used by the assistant and the

Bobo doll itself. Perhaps unsurprisingly to us now, but groundbreaking for its time, Dr. Bandura and his team found that the children who witnessed the aggressive behavior resulting in a reward quickly went to work brutalizing the doll in many of the same ways they observed previously, despite not being trained or told to do so. In this manner, the mere act of associating or conditioning the perceived behavior with a prospective reward proved more than enough to shape their behavior drastically. Conversely, those children who did not witness the behavior or see a reprimand for the aggressive behavior were far less likely to display aggression towards the Bobo doll.

Of course, the implications of this research extend far beyond toys, dolls, and children. Social learning also serves an important role in learning within organizational settings. One of the most powerful tools leaders and trainers have at their disposal is behavioral modeling. Organizational leaders, managers, and training facilitators frequently use modeling to set an example for acceptable behavior by first demonstrating those behaviors themselves. The reason this modeling works is by virtue of senior staff members' status, success, and power, which serves to incentivize imitation from their subordinates in anticipation of a positive outcome (Brown, et al., 2005) in much the same way as those children imitated their authority figures during Bandura's experiments. However, keep in mind that modeling and imitation do not always result in positive outcomes, and undesirable traits may also be unwittingly or purposely imitated for many of the same reasons previously mentioned (Manz & Sims, 1981).

Comparing Social Constructivism and Social Learning Theory

Social constructivism is the knowledge that develops from how people interact with each other, their culture, and society at large. Social learning theory states that individuals learn through observing, imitating, and modeling others' behavior. So comparing these two, it is best to distinguish them based on focus: social constructivism focuses on acquiring *new knowledge*; social learning theory focuses on *changing behavior*. This is a subtle, yet important, distinction.

Situated Cognition

Compared to classroom/school forms of instruction, workplace learning often involves learners immediately applying new knowledge to resolve organizational needs that generate tangible value for the organization. This leads us to situated cognition, which posits that cognitive processes, such as thinking, learning, and problem-solving, are deeply influenced by the context or "situation" in which they occur (Nathan & Sawyer, 2014). Rather than viewing cognition as an abstract and independent mental process, situated cognition emphasizes that cognitive activities are intricately tied to the physical, social, and cultural environment in which they take place.

Environmental Influences

Situated cognition builds on Vygotsky's concept of internalization. Born out of ethnographic work on workplace learning and apprenticeship conducted in the 80s and 90s, Vygotsky's ideas expanded beyond the transfer of socially mediated interpersonal to intrapersonal knowledge generation. Instead of envisioning learning as a process occurring during activity and sustained by relationships between practitioners (Gherardi et al., 1998), learners enculture themselves to a broader community of practice, that subsequently enables the community's foundational principles, tools, and beliefs to live on and grow

through the inductee's membership and contributions back into the community (Brown et al., 1989).

Communities of Practice

A community of practice (CoP) is a group of people who share a common interest, domain, or area of expertise and who interact regularly to learn from each other, collaborate, and collectively develop their knowledge and skills in that particular domain. Such group interactions can be formal or informal. CoPs are characterized by their voluntary nature, a sense of shared identity, and a commitment to improving their practices or solving problems related to their shared interest.

The process of joining a community of practice is often gradual, with new members taking on low-risk, but nonetheless authentic, tasks while working under the guidance of a more experienced mentor who gradually shares not only the relevant knowledge, ideals, and customs of their craft with the pupil (Lave & Wenger, 1991) but an entirely new way of *thinking* (Collins et al., 1991); which explains why CoPs are considered forms of *cognitive* apprenticeship. As such, any learning that occurs is inseparable from the individual actions and interpersonal, environmental conditions in which that knowledge was initially developed (Brown et al., 1989).

As mentioned previously, the knowledge shared via the apprenticeships and larger community of practice is purpose-built for accomplishing practical tasks related to the concerns of that particular community; this however does not necessarily mean those practices are the most efficient, or useful given another situational context. Imagine suddenly asking a car mechanic to design an engine for a new car; how well do you expect them to perform at this task? Certainly, the mechanic understands how an engine works, what parts go into its function, and perhaps even how to assemble and disassemble one. However, their understanding of what an engine *is* remains rooted in the context of their practice as a mechanic, not an engineer, and vice-versa. That is, plenty of skilled engineers may not know how to change their car's oil or swap out a taillight despite their extensive knowledge of mechanics and electronics.

To further illustrate this point, let us consider an example of employees from different backgrounds collaborating while trying to solve the same problem. In one instance, workers on an electronic assembly line complained to the engineering department over the phone that their component placer machine was "drifting" and gradually placing components further out of tolerance (Tyre & Von Hippel, 1997). Based on the phone conversation, the engineer on call quickly surmised the assembly workers must be incorrectly programming the machine. However, further attempts to rectify the problem proved futile until eventually the engineer decided to visit the floor himself. Upon arriving and looking over the machine, he immediately realized that two of the screws attached to the placer's camera were loose, and based on those embedded clues in the environment, he quickly discovered the appropriate solution.

An important note worth mentioning here is these moments of thinking and problem-solving are *transitory* approximations, meaning they are temporary, best guesses based on the immediate clues around us, and that our knowledge is limited to the exact set of circumstances occurring, which means that information obtained from one instance may not transfer effectively to another (Lave & Wenger, 1991; Elsbach et al., 2005). This is because the consolidated understanding, or solution, is constructed to fit the exact circumstances in which it was initially learned and applied. For our engineer, his job did not normally require visiting the shop floor, and therefore his approximation for what was causing this transitory problem is inadvertently influenced by his past experiences and training.

Examples like this also demonstrate how embedded clues in a given context tell our brains how to think and behave in a certain situation. This varies considerably from the type of uniform worn, and the tools used, to the individual's idiosyncratic schemata and expectations for what their job and others' roles entail.

So, why does human cognition rely so much on environmental cues and context when thinking about problems? The reason, naturally, is due to our brains, or more specifically the limited storage and processing capacity of working memory. Because the brain is functionally limited in its ability to actively process *all* of the relevant information available to it, whether that information is coming from sensory perception or memory recall—your mind, or prefrontal cortex, never has all the information necessary to make the best decision possible—there is always going to be some guesswork involved.

This concept of bounded rationality requires us to consider the mental shortcuts, or heuristics, that humans use to balance the need for accuracy with rapid response times. Herbert Simon, the originator of this idea, explains it best:

> Of all the knowledge, attitudes, and values stored in a human memory, only a very small fraction are evoked in any given situation. Thus, an individual can assume a variety of roles when these are evoked by appropriate circumstances, each of which may interact only weakly with the others.
>
> (Simon, 1997, p. 158)

In evolutionary terms, it is not enough to merely recognize a tiger hiding in the bush, you also need enough time to run away. In most instances, heuristic decision-making is *good enough*, particularly in cases where the need to move quickly outweighs the need for absolute accuracy or where there is already a low level of predictability (Gigerenzer & Gaissmaier, 2011). However, heuristics can also lead to poor choices that impact performance and project outcomes if the solution does not adequately address the problem at hand or is founded on.

There are three main ways to overcome this problem. First, whenever training employees, be sure the circumstances of the learning experience are *authentic* to the environment in which they will be applied (Brown et al., 1989). That means using the same tools, lingo, and embedded clues during training that will be accessible to them during their actual job. Second, welcome experienced employees into the learning process to share their thought process *explicitly* with novices; that means visually showing and verbally explaining the rationale of how they think and perform the actions of their role (Collins et al., 1991). Finally, the third tool is to employ communities of practice to help overcome some of the more complex challenges situated cognition presents on the organizational scale.

As explained previously, communities of practice serve as a consolidated repository of knowledge obtained by a community of learners and practitioners over an extended period of time (often across several years to entire generations). In organizations, this often emerges as functional or voluntary workgroups with leadership emerging from within the community via seniority and where employees have opportunities to share knowledge and work collaboratively on projects (Wenger et al., 2002). These communities serve many functions, but most of all they enable information to readily travel across bureaucratic boundaries, store institutional memory, consolidate efforts to address similar problems across the organization, prevent reworking previously solved issues, and encourage innovation through the sharing of new knowledge and differing perspectives (Lesser & Storck, 2001). In this way, communities of practice are uniquely capable of reducing the reliance on individually situated and occasionally flawed problem-solving by enabling the sharing of new knowledge, fresh perspectives, and possible solutions (Wenger, 1999).

Hopefully, at this point, you can see that situated cognition has broad implications for workplace learning and performance, as it provides a framework for understanding many diverse organizational phenomena, such as why team members with different professional backgrounds struggle to collaborate effectively (Elsbach et al., 2005), or why learners more easily recall information in an environment or context similar to where they first learned it (Godden & Baddeley, 1975). While there are no doubt complexities and challenges to working within this orientation, those who take the time to employ its adaptive and eclectic toolkit will not only be capable of improving learning and performance in a small setting through scaffolding, mentorships, and demonstrations but also on a much broader, organizational level through communities of practice.

Developing CoPs within an organization can be a valuable strategy for fostering knowledge sharing, collaboration, and expertise development among employees. Below I provide a list of ways in which organizations can create vibrant internal CoPs that facilitate learning, innovation, and knowledge sharing among employees, ultimately benefiting the organization as a whole:

1. **Identify the purpose and domain:** First, clearly define the purpose and focus of the CoP. Identify the specific domain or subject matter relevant to the CoP's goals, thus ensuring that members share a common interest.
2. **Identify potential members:** Identify employees who have expertise or a keen interest in the chosen domain. Consider involving members from various departments or teams to ensure diverse perspectives.
3. **Leadership and facilitation:** Appoint a leader or facilitator who is passionate about the domain and is responsible for organizing and guiding CoP activities. This leader can be an experienced employee or someone with subject matter expertise. Finding a sponsor who is senior in level is advantageous to the CoP's success as well.
4. **Create a platform for communication:** Establish a dedicated platform for CoP members to communicate, share resources, and collaborate. This can be a digital platform or a physical meeting space.
5. **Encourage knowledge sharing:** Create a culture of knowledge sharing within the CoP. Encourage members to share their expertise, best practices, and resources. Use various formats, such as presentations, workshops, or discussion threads, to facilitate knowledge sharing.
6. **Collaborative projects and activities:** Plan and initiate collaborative projects or activities related to the CoP's domain. These projects provide practical learning experiences and foster teamwork. Encourage members to work together on solving real-world challenges or creating innovative solutions.
7. **Documentation and resources:** Maintain a repository of resources, documents, and references related to the CoP's domain/topic. Ensure that these resources are easily accessible and well-organized (because disorganization is a major pitfall to avoid).
8. **Evaluate and adapt:** Periodically assess the effectiveness of the CoP in meeting its objectives. Gather feedback from members and use it to make improvements. Adapt the CoP's activities and focus as needed based on the evolving needs and goals of the organization.
9. **Scale and expand**: Consider expanding the CoP concept to other relevant domains or areas within the company as the organization grows and evolves.
10. **Promote inclusivity:** Ensure that the CoP is inclusive and open to all interested employees. Avoid exclusivity or creating barriers to entry.
11. **Provide resources and support:** Allocate resources and support for CoPs, such as budget for training, guest speakers, or technology tools. Encourage senior leadership to endorse and support CoPs as part of the company's culture.

Psychological Safety

In any discussion of social learning, but especially one dealing with organizational settings, it is prudent to introduce psychological safety. *Psychological safety* refers to the perception that an individual's work environment is safe for taking interpersonal risks (Edmondson & Lei, 2014; Newman et al., 2017). It involves feeling confident that one will not face negative consequences or judgment when expressing ideas, sharing concerns, or taking risks within a group or organizational setting. In psychologically safe environments, individuals believe that they can be themselves without fear of retribution or embarrassment (Edmondson & Lei, 2014). Key elements of psychological safety include the following:

- **Open communication:** Team members feel free to express their thoughts, ideas, and opinions without fear of criticism or punishment. This encourages open and honest communication.
- **Risk-taking:** Individuals feel comfortable taking calculated risks, sharing innovative ideas, and proposing new solutions without the fear of negative consequences.
- **Interpersonal trust:** Team members trust each other, believing that their colleagues have good intentions and will not harm them, either professionally or personally.
- **Respectful environment:** The work environment is characterized by mutual respect, where individuals value each other's contributions, regardless of differences in opinions, background, or expertise.
- **Constructive feedback:** Feedback is provided in a constructive and supportive manner. Individuals feel that feedback is aimed at helping them grow and improve rather than criticizing or blaming them.
- **Empowerment:** Team members feel empowered to voice concerns, challenge the status quo, and contribute to decision-making processes. They believe their perspectives are valued.
- **Freedom to be oneself:** Individuals can bring their authentic selves to the workplace, expressing their personalities, values, and beliefs without fear of discrimination or exclusion.
- **Learning from mistakes:** Failure is viewed as an opportunity for learning and improvement rather than as a reason for punishment. This mindset encourages experimentation and innovation.

Psychological safety is critical for fostering a positive and productive learning environment. Research indicates that teams and organizations with high levels of psychological safety are more likely to be innovative, creative, and resilient (Newman et al., 2017; Carmeli et al., 2010). When individuals feel safe to share their thoughts, take risks, and make mistakes amongst their peers, evidence shows this leads to better problem-solving, increased collaboration, and overall higher levels of job satisfaction (Frazier et al., 2017; Chen et al., 2014).

Application of This Chapter

Professionals should leverage the principles of social constructivism, ZPD, and social learning theory to create effective learning experiences that capitalize on the power of social interactions and collaborative learning. I list below several strategies to leverage the principles of these two social learning theories into one's practice in face-to-face settings:

1 **Encourage collaborative activities:** Incorporate group projects, discussions, and collaborative exercises into the learning materials. These activities promote interaction among learners, allowing them to share knowledge, perspectives, and experiences. This can enhance understanding and retention of the subject matter.
2 **Peer modeling:** Use peer modeling as a teaching tool. Showcase examples of successful learners or peers who have mastered the content. Learners often find it easier to relate to and learn from their peers, making this an effective way to demonstrate desired behaviors or skills.
3 **Facilitate peer teaching:** Encourage learners to take on the role of teachers by having them explain concepts or demonstrate skills to their peers. Peer teaching not only reinforces their understanding but also allows them to receive feedback and alternative perspectives from fellow learners.
4 **Discussion forums and social media:** Create online discussion forums or utilize social media platforms to foster discussions, knowledge sharing, and networking among learners. These platforms can serve as virtual communities where learners can exchange ideas and support each other's learning journeys.
5 **Expert interviews:** Integrate interviews or guest lectures from subject matter experts or individuals with relevant experiences. Learners can benefit from exposure to different viewpoints and real-world applications of the content, providing a social context for their learning.
6 **Feedback and peer assessment:** Implement peer assessment and feedback mechanisms where learners evaluate each other's work or contributions. This not only helps learners develop critical evaluation skills but also encourages constructive interactions and collaboration.
7 **Collaborative tools:** Utilize online collaboration tools and platforms that enable learners to work together on projects, share resources, and communicate in real time. Tools like Slack, Google Workspace, or dedicated learning management systems (LMS) can facilitate collaborative learning.
8 **Group problem solving:** Present complex problems or scenarios that require group analysis and solutions. This encourages learners to work together, share insights, and apply their collective knowledge to find answers, mirroring real-world problem-solving situations.
9 **Supportive learning communities:** Foster a sense of belonging and community among learners. Encourage them to support each other, share their challenges and successes, and provide emotional support when needed. An inclusive and supportive learning community can boost motivation and engagement.
10 **Scaffolded learning experiences:** Gradually increase the complexity of collaborative activities to match the learners' evolving skills and knowledge. This scaffolding approach ensures that learners build on their previous social learning experiences and progressively develop expertise.

Furthermore, leveraging social constructivism and social learning theory in remote work environments can enhance collaboration, skill development, and knowledge sharing among remote teams. Here are four strategies to apply these theories effectively in a remote work context:

1 **Peer learning communities:** Foster peer learning groups or communities of practice within your remote team. These smaller groups can focus on specific topics or skills and meet regularly to share insights, best practices, and resources. Encourage members to take turns leading discussions or sharing their expertise.

2 **Mentorship programs:** Establish remote mentorship programs where experienced team members can guide and support newer employees. Mentorship can be conducted through virtual meetings, email, or messaging apps. Pairing less experienced team members with mentors can accelerate skill development and knowledge transfer.
3 **Collaborative projects:** Assign collaborative projects that require team members to work together and share expertise. These projects can simulate real-world challenges and provide opportunities for social learning as team members pool their knowledge and skills to achieve common goals.
4 **Knowledge sharing sessions:** Organize virtual knowledge sharing sessions where team members can present their expertise on specific topics. This can be in the form of webinars, lunch-and-learns, or regular knowledge-sharing meetings. Rotate presenters to diversify the learning experience.

By integrating these strategies into practice, professionals can harness the principles of social learning theory to create engaging and effective learning environments that capitalize on the social interactions and collaborative opportunities among learners. This approach not only enhances the learning experience but also prepares learners for real-world contexts where collaboration and social learning are often essential.

References

Amineh, R. J., & Asl, H. D. (2015). Review of constructivism and social constructivism. *Journal of Social Sciences, Literature and Languages*, 1(1), 9–16.

Bandura, A., Ross, D., & Ross, S. A. (1961). Transmission of aggression through imitation of aggressive models. *The Journal of Abnormal and Social Psychology*, 63(3), 575.

Brown, J. S., Collins, A., Duguid, S. (1989). Situated cognition and the culture of learning. *Educational Researcher*, 18(1), 32–42.

Brown, M. E., Treviño, L. K., & Harrison, D. A. (2005). Ethical leadership: A social learning perspective for construct development and testing. *Organizational Behavior and Human Decision Processes*, 97(2), 117–134.

Carmeli, A., Reiter-Palmon, R., & Ziv, E. (2010). Inclusive leadership and employee involvement in creative tasks in the workplace: The mediating role of psychological safety. *Creativity Research Journal*, 22, 250–260.

Chen, C., Liao, J., & Wen, P. (2014). Why does formal mentoring matter? The mediating role of psychological safety and the moderating role of power distance orientation in the Chinese context. *International Journal of Human Resource Management*, 25, 1112–1130.

Collins, A., Brown, J. S., & Holum, A. (1991). Cognitive apprenticeship: Making thinking visible. *American Educator*, 15(3), 6–11.

Frazier, M. L., Fainshmidt, S., Klinger, R. L., Pezeshkan, A., & Vracheva, V. (2017). Psychological safety: A meta-analytic review and extension. *Personnel Psychology*, 70(1), 113–165.

Gherardi, S., Nicolini, D., & Odella, F. (1998). Toward a social understanding of how people learn in organizations: The notion of situated curriculum. *Management Learning*, 29(3), 273–297.

Gigerenzer, G., & Gaissmaier, W. (2011). Heuristic decision making. *Annual Review of Psychology*, 62, 451–482.

Godden, D. R., & Baddeley, A. D. (1975). Context-dependent memory in two natural environments: On land and underwater. *British Journal of Psychology*, 66(3), 325–331.

Edmondson, A. C., & Lei, Z. (2014). Psychological safety: The history, renaissance, and future of an interpersonal construct. *Annual Review of Organizational Psychology and Organizational Behavior*, 1(1), 23–43.

Elsbach, K. D., Barr, P. S., & Hargadon, A. B. (2005). Identifying situated cognition in organizations. *Organization Science*, 16(4), 422–433.

Lave, J., & Wenger, E. (1991). *Situated learning: Legitimate peripheral participation.* Cambridge University Press.

Lesser, E. L., & Storck, J. (2001). Communities of practice and organizational performance. *IBM Systems Journal*, 40(4), 831–841.

Manz, C. C., & Sims, H. P. (1981). Vicarious learning: The influence of modeling on organizational behavior. *Academy of Management Review*, 6(1), 105–113.

Nathan, M. J., & Sawyer, R. K. (2014). Foundations of the learning sciences. In R. K. Sawyer (Ed.), *The Cambridge handbook of the learning sciences* (pp. 21–43). Cambridge University Press.

Newman, A., Donohue, R., & Eva, N. (2017). Psychological safety: A systematic review of the literature. *Human Resource Management Review*, 27(3), 521–535.

Simon, H. A. (1997). *Administrative behavior.* Simon and Schuster.

Subotnik, R. F., & Jarvin, L. (2005). Beyond expertise: Conceptions of giftedness as great performance. In R. J. Sternberg & J. E. Davidson (Eds.), *Conceptions of giftedness* (2nd ed., pp. 343–357). Cambridge University Press.

Tyre, M. J., & Von Hippel, E. (1997). The situated nature of adaptive learning in organizations. *Organization Science*, 8 (1), 71–83.

Vygotsky, L. S. (1978). *Mind in society: The development of higher psychological processes.* Harvard University Press.

Wenger, E. (1999). *Communities of practice: Learning, meaning, and identity.* Cambridge University Press.

Wenger, E., McDermott, R., & Snyder, W. (2002). *Cultivating communities of practice: A guide to managing knowledge.* Harvard Business School Press.

Westbrook, L. (2006). Mental models: a theoretical overview and preliminary study. *Journal of Information Science*, 32(6), 563–579.

11 Attitude and Emotion in Learning

Attitude and Mindset

An individual's *attitude* represents his or her feelings and regard for a particular person, event, or situation. One's attitude is something that is learned and developed over time, and reflects his/her values, belief-system, and past experiences. Research has demonstrated that a learner's attitude toward learning is an extremely strong predictor of engagement and success (Erdoğdu, 2020). For example, an individual's attitude toward learning in the cognitive dimension is seen in their willingness to learn; in the behavioral dimension, a learner's attitude will typically reflect their participation in relevant activities (Finlay, 2006; Fredricks et al., 2004).

Closely related to a person's attitude is the concept of *mindset*. A *mindset* is a core belief or set of assumptions we have about a domain, that serves to orient us toward expectations, explanations, and goals (Crum et al., 2013). Mindsets shape both our thinking and behavior. As such, a learner's mindset can play a critical role in determining the rate of learning and growth that he or she experiences. For more on mindsets, see the psychological research work of Dweck (2015, 2016) and Crum et al. (2013).

Growth Mindset

Recall from Chapter 2 the important role of *grit*, or resilience, in order to accomplish long-term goals. One mindset in particular that is closely related to grit and has received increasing scholarship recently is known as a *growth mindset*. A growth mindset is one in which the individual believes in their untapped potential and the possibility of growing and developing (Dweck 2015, 2016). In essence, an individual with a growth mindset tells themselves, "My ability is not fixed, I can improve (X) by working. I can achieve (X) through effort." Research by Moser et al. (2011) showed high significance between a person's mindset type (i.e. growth vs. fixed) and their response to making an error (known as *error positivity* (Pe)). Stated simply, those with a growth mindset demonstrated awareness to divert attention toward an error that occurred—that is, they did not shy away from the error, they "owned it." These individuals also demonstrated a pattern of better post-error performance compared to individuals with a fixed mindset.

Additionally, research by Dr. Yeager at the University of Texas–Austin suggests the combination of two simultaneous mindsets (1) "I can improve through meaningful effort," and (2) "stress is enhancing," show very positive, synergistic effects (Yeager et al., 2022). They reached a series of compelling findings, but two stand out for our purposes. For individuals possessing both mindsets simultaneously (i.e. a growth mindset and stress-is-enhancing mindset), they discovered not only a reduction in daily cortisol levels but also noticeable improvements in memory performance.

DOI: 10.4324/9781003593607-15

The Role of Emotion

"Human emotions, such as anxiety, depression, fear, joy, and laughter, profoundly impact psychological and physiological processes" (Savage et al., 2017, p. 345). Research has found that emotions play a significant role in the learning process (Pekrun & Linnenbrink-Garcia, 2014; Schutz & Pekrun, 2007). After reviewing several decades of relevant literature on *The Influences of Emotion on Learning and Memory*, Tyng and colleagues concluded the following:

> Emotion has a substantial influence on the cognitive processes in humans, including perception, attention, learning, memory, reasoning, and problem solving. Emotion has a particularly strong influence on attention, especially modulating the selectivity of attention as well as motivating action and behavior. This attentional and executive control is intimately linked to learning processes, as intrinsically limited attentional capacities are better focused on relevant information. Emotion also facilitates encoding and helps retrieval of information efficiently. However, the effects of emotion on learning and memory are not always univalent, as studies have reported that emotion either enhances or impairs learning and long-term memory (LTM) retention, depending on a range of factors.
>
> (Tyng et al., 2017, p. 1)

To be clear, the relationship between emotion and cognition is bidirectional (see Figure 11.1). That is, our emotions impact our cognitive processes, and our cognitive processes impact our emotions.

Figure 11.1 Bidirectional relationship between emotion and cognition

Three processes in particular—attention, motivation, and emotion—are tightly intertwined and it is the amygdala which links them together (Raymond, 2009; Li et al., 2020). Recall from Chapter 2 that the amygdala is the brain structure that processes our emotions. This is represented by the amygdala being activated during the encoding of emotionally charged information, which correlates with a significantly improved ability to recall those events later: "Activation of the amygdala during the encoding of emotionally arousing information (both pleasant/unpleasant) has been reported that correlates with subsequent recall" (Tyng et al., 2017, pp. 7–8). Additionally, the amygdala also interacts with cortical regions to influence other aspects of memory, in a phenomenon known as ***arousal-mediated memory consolidation***. Regarding this phenomenon, LaBar (2007) stated:

> These include the encoding and consolidation of pleasant and unpleasant arousing events into long-term memory, the narrowing of focus on central emotional information, the retrieval of prior emotional events and contexts, and the subjective experience of recollection and emotional intensity during retrieval. Along with other mechanisms that do not involve the amygdala, these functions ensure that significant life events leave a lasting impression in memory.
>
> (LaBar, 2007, p. 173)

With the amygdala playing such a vital role in both the formation of memory and in other cognitive functions, it may come as no surprise that learning is also greatly influenced by a learner's emotional state. What can be best described as emotional thought, the consolidation of decision making, morality, memory, learning, and social interaction under the shared umbrella of emotional processing provides a more nuanced understanding of how cognitive processes influence, and are in turn influenced by, a learner's emotional state (Immordino-Yang & Damasio, 2007).

> Learning requires a marriage of several vital components: attention, motivation, and emotion give rise to the prioritization and selection of information … Attention can be described as a set of mechanisms that enable perceptual processing of stimuli and can be seen as the main gatekeeper for visual awareness … Motivation designates a goal, or the order of goals needed to perform a complex task, and guides attention. Emotion can influence and change the processes of *both* attention and motivation … It has been generally shown that emotional stimuli engage and hold attention more than neutral or novel stimuli …
>
> (Li et al., 2020, p. 221)

In other words, emotion directly impacts several key aspects of the learning process: motivation, attention, memory, and decision making (Immordino-Yang & Damasio, 2007).

In general, positive emotions stimulate motivation, enhance attention, and strengthen memory. Conversely, negative emotions, at best do none of these, or at worst serve to demotivate the learner, undermine attention, and complicate the learning process (Fredrickson & Branigan, 2005). To be clear, however, emotionally arousing events that a person experiences dominate the long-term memory; the more emotionally arousing the event or experience, the more profound the memory (see Dolcos et al., 2005). While there are countless emotions from which to choose, the next sections will consider how *happiness, humor, stress, anxiety*, and *fear* each impact adult learning.

Happiness

The key impact that happiness has on learning is in improving learner attention and motivation (Li et al., 2020). Research conducted by Fredrickson and Branigan (2005) found that positive emotions like joy and contentment can enhance attention. Further, Omar et al. (2013) discovered a symbiotic relationship: *learners who are motivated to learn were happy, while those who were happy were motivated to learn.* Research has also demonstrated that happiness and joy greatly enhance the memory process. Hamann (2001) found that these types of positive emotions stimulate arousal that directly impacts the encoding (i.e. consolidating) of information into one's long-term memory. The emotional context of such happy memories significantly enhances the ability to then recall the memories later (Sommer et al., 2008).

Humor

According to research, laughter induces the brain to release a powerful combination of healthy hormones that include endorphins, oxytocin (which causes feelings of bonding, connection, and sexual intimacy with another person), and a reduction of the stress hormone cortisol, thus making a person calmer (see Vedantam, 2021; Aaker & Bagdonas, 2021). What's more impressive, research has shown that laughter causes our brain to release each of these at the same time. In a sense, laughter is akin to exercising, meditating,

and sexual intimacy *all at once* (Vedantam, 2021)! In this way, laughter can serve as a means to bring people together.

For our interests, research has found that humor promotes and enhances learning (Lujan & DiCarlo, 2016). After reviewing four decades worth of research on humor's impact on learning, Banas et al. (2011) concluded that humor is highly effective at achieving the sustained attraction of learners' attention, as well as increasing learner motivation. But the caveat is that the humor must be directly related to the subject-matter being learned (Savage et al., 2017). In a seminal study, learners who were taught with topic-relevant humor retained more information when compared to control groups who were taught without humor. In fact, the use of humor when giving examples significantly increased recall/retrieval for those concepts that leveraged humorous examples (Ziv, 2014).

With regard to the specific amount of humor, research has shown that 3–4 humorous examples per hour, used intermittently and at a cadence that is not predictable or prescribed, is ideal. The evidence suggests doing this yields better results than a regular schedule of humor. Furthermore, for instructors and facilitators, self-effacing humor is especially effective because it informs learners that the instructor is okay with making mistakes. In this manner, humor has been found to be a significant aid in fostering an appropriate and honest relationship between teacher/facilitator and learner (Claus et al., 2012).

Stress

Stress is typically considered a negative emotional state, in which cortisol (the stress hormone) is released. However, this is not exactly so; there is nuance to the impact of stress. Vogel and Schwabe (2016) discovered that intensity and duration of stress can either impede or promote learning and memory. Specifically, they found that stress that is mild and acute was found to facilitate learning and enhance cognitive performance. (Recall in Chapter 2 that the discomfort from *resistance*, and even *mistakes*, is productive in the learning process.) Conversely, they also found that excessive and chronic stress impaired learning and overall cognitive performance, including the accuracy of memory recall (Brainerd et al., 2008).

Vogel and Schwabe (2016) also found the effects of stress on memory vary depending on the timing and duration of the stress as well, such as experiencing prolonged stress before encoding (e.g. living at home in a chronically stressful environment) significantly impairs the formation and integration of new memories. However, *short-term stress* shortly before or after instruction tended to enhance subsequent retrieval performance. In sharp contrast, stress before memory retrieval impairs the recall of previously learned information. In general, chronic stress is a detriment to learning and best kept to a minimum. That said, in manageable and short bursts, stress can also serve as a powerful tool for improving attention and learning performance.

Anxiety

Nolan and Bergin (2016) reviewed several scholarly articles on anxiety and learning and concluded that a meaningful relationship exists between feelings of anxiety and a learner's performance. They further theorized that during the learning event itself, three factors are most likely to contribute towards feelings of anxiety: (1) task complexity, (2) notification of errors, and (3) collaborative learning. Regarding task complexity in particular, Owens et al. (2014) found that working memory capacity was proportional to the strength of the feelings of anxiety. In other words, when the cognitive load was manageable, the anxiety felt

was low and cognitive performance was minimally impacted. However, when cognitive overload was reached, the level of anxiety learners experienced increased significantly and as a result, cognitive performance suffered. King et al. (2011) found that anxiety often leads learners to feeling paralyzed, or "stuck," during encoding and/or recall.

Fear

Closely related to stress and anxiety is the role of fear in the learning process:

> Fear usually brings about anxiety and causes stress, but it is different from both. In the making of fear memory, the predominant factors are a threat and the reaction to it; this is not always or necessarily the case in anxiety and stress.
>
> (Izquierdo et al., 2016, p. 696)

Fear memory is formed in the hippocampus and amygdala, but also involves the circuitry of the prefrontal cortex (Izquierdo et al., 2016). As discussed in Chapter 3, fear is an emotion with a powerful impact on memory due to its role in threat-avoidance and, ultimately, our survival. Izquierdo et al. (2016) stated the following:

> Fear learning gives rise to some of the strongest, most detailed and longer-lasting memories, because in the interface between their acquisition and the subsequent consolidation there is a high degree of emotional arousal that is known to enhance memory consolidation ... and, to an extent, reconsolidation ...
>
> (Izquierdo et al., 2016, p. 698)

Emotional Intelligence

Emotional intelligence (or EQ for "emotional quotient") refers to the ability to understand and manage one's own emotions effectively, as well as the ability to perceive, understand, and respond to the emotions of others (Salovey & Mayer, 1990; Goleman, 1995). Put another way, EQ involves the KSAs that enable individuals to navigate their emotions and interact with the emotions of those around them in a healthy and productive manner. Emotional intelligence consists of three fundamental components: *self-awareness, social-awareness*, and *relationship management.*

Self-awareness

Self-awareness is the ability to recognize and understand (1) one's own emotions, values, and motivators, and (2) the impact they have on you. Those with high self-awareness know their strengths, weaknesses, motivators, and triggers. High self-awareness involves recognition of one's own emotional states. A key aspect of self-awareness is self-management (also known as self-regulation). This refers to the capacity to manage and control one's emotional reactions and behavior (versus allowing them to control you), especially in challenging or stressful situations. This capacity very much includes motivation management, which is the ability to harness and direct emotions to achieve personal and professional goals, while staying persistent in the face of challenges or obstacles. Self-awareness and self-management can be developed by seeking feedback and through mindfulness practices such as reflection and journaling.

Social Awareness

Social awareness refers to *empathy*, which is the ability to perceive and understand the emotions, needs, and perspectives of others, and to respond with appropriate sensitivity. Those with high social awareness go beyond recognition; they genuinely care about the emotional needs of others and act with empathy. Social awareness can be developed through (1) active listening, paying attention to non-verbal cues, (2) placing themselves in the other's point of view before responding, and (3) in team interactions showing appreciation and recognizing the emotions of others (Goleman, 1995).

Relationship Management

Relationship management is the capacity to build and maintain healthy relationships, communicate effectively, resolve conflicts, and foster collaboration with others. Individuals who are strong in managing relationships build trust and communicate with clarity. To develop relationship management, individuals should communicate clearly and with compassion, and foster a positive team culture by celebrating wins.

Emotional intelligence plays a critical role in many aspects of life, including personal relationships, leadership, communication, and decision-making. People with higher emotional intelligence tend to exhibit better interpersonal skills, are more adaptable, and can effectively manage stress and challenges. The key for our purposes is that emotional intelligence can indeed be developed and improved through reflection, practice, and learning from personal or vicarious experiences (Goleman, 1995; Serrat, 2017, pp. 329–339).

Application of This Chapter

Emotions play a profound role in the process of learning. When individuals experience positive emotions such as happiness, humor, or engagement, it enhances their ability to absorb and retain information. And in short bursts, stress can enhance memory as well. On the contrary, negative emotions like anxiety, prolonged stress, and fear can impair cognitive functions and inhibit the retrieval of previously learned information.

Therefore, professionals should aim to leverage the impact of emotions on learning to create more effective and engaging learning experiences. Below are several key strategies to consider increase the efficacy and engagement level of the learning experiences you design.

- **Emotional engagement:** aim to evoke positive emotions like curiosity, interest, and enthusiasm in learners. This can be achieved through well-crafted content, storytelling, and multimedia elements that resonate with learners on a personal level. Engaging scenarios, relatable examples, and real-world applications can stimulate emotional connections to the subject matter.
- **Establish a safe learning environment:** reducing anxiety and stress is crucial for optimal learning. Professionals should seek to create a supportive and non-threatening learning environment where learners feel comfortable asking questions, making mistakes, and taking risks. Providing clear guidelines, constructive feedback, and resources for managing emotional challenges can enhance the overall experience.
- **Personalization:** recognize that different learners may have varying emotional responses to the same content. Tailor instructional materials to accommodate diverse emotional needs and preferences. Allow for choices and flexibility in the learning process, enabling learners to pursue topics and approaches that resonate with their emotions.

- **Storytelling and narrative:** storytelling can be a powerful tool to engage emotions. Incorporate narratives that connect with learners on an emotional level. Stories can help contextualize information, making it more relatable and memorable. They can also create emotional arcs that mirror the learning journey, fostering a sense of accomplishment and satisfaction. (We will discuss the power of storytelling in greater depth in the next chapter.)
- **Active learning and interactivity:** encourage active learning through interactive exercises, discussions, and collaborative activities. Active participation can generate a sense of achievement and emotional investment in the learning process. Gamification and simulation can also add an element of fun and challenge, eliciting positive emotions.
- **Feedback and recognition:** providing timely and constructive feedback can boost learners' *self-esteem* and *motivation*. Recognize and celebrate their achievements and progress, reinforcing positive emotions. Peer recognition and social reinforcement can also play a significant role in emotional engagement.
- **Reflection and self-awareness:** incorporate opportunities for learners to *reflect* on their emotional responses to the content and their learning journey. Encourage self-awareness and metacognition, allowing learners to recognize and manage their emotions effectively.
- **Emotional support resources:** offer resources and support for learners who may be experiencing negative emotions, such as frustration or anxiety. This could include access to counseling services, mindfulness exercises, or strategies for managing stress.

Incorporating these strategies into our professional practice can enhance the emotional impact of learning, making it a more enjoyable, meaningful, and effective experience for learners. By acknowledging—dare I say "owning"—the role of emotions in learning, professionals can significantly help learners connect with, encode, and retrieve information more effectively and efficiently.

References

Aaker, J., & Bagdonas, N. (2021). *Humor, seriously: Why humor is a secret weapon in business and life (and how anyone can harness it. Even you.)*. Currency.

Banas, J. A., Dunbar, N., Rodriguez, D., & Liu, S. J. (2011). A review of humor in educational settings: Four decades of research. *Communication Education*, 60(1), 115–144.

Brainerd, C. J., Stein, L. M., Silveira, R. A., Rohenkohl, G., & Reyna, V. F. (2008). How does negative emotion cause false memories? *Psychological Science*, 19(9), 919–925.

Cahill, L., & McGaugh, J. L. (1998). Mechanisms of emotional arousal and lasting declarative memory. *Trends Neuroscience*, 21, 294–299, 1998.

Claus, C. J., Booth-Butterfield, M., & Chory, R. M. (2012). The relationship between instructor misbehaviors and student antisocial behavioral alteration techniques: The roles of instructor attractiveness, humor, and relational closeness. *Communication Education*, 61(2), 161–183.

Crum, A. J., Salovey, P., & Achor, S. (2013). Rethinking stress: the role of mindsets in determining the stress response. *Journal of Personality and Social Psychology*, 104(4), 716.

Dolcos, F., LaBar, K.S., & Cabeza, R. (2005). Remembering one year later: Role of the amygdala and the medial temporal lobe memory system in retrieving emotional memories. *Proceedings of the National Academy of Sciences, USA*, 102, 2626–2631.

Dweck, C. (2015). Carol Dweck revisits the growth Mindset. *Education Week*, 35(5), 20–24.

Dweck, C. (2016). What having a "growth mindset" actually means. *Harvard Business Review*, 13 (2), 2–5.

Erdoğdu, M. Y. (2020). The roles of attitudes towards learning and opposite sex as a predictor of school engagement: Mixed or single gender education? *Palgrave Communications*, 6(1), 1–9.

Finlay, K. A. (2006). Quantifying school engagement. https://schoolengagement.org/wp-content/uploads/2021/02/QuantifyingSchoolEngagementResearchReport.pdf.

Fredricks, J. A., Blumenfeld, P. C., & Paris, A. H. (2004). School engagement: Potential of the concept, state of the evidence. *Review of Educational Research*, 74(1), 59–109.

Fredrickson, B. L., & Branigan, C. (2005). Positive emotions broaden the scope of attention and thought-action repertoires. *Cognition & Emotion*, 19(3), 313–332.

Goleman, D. P. (1995). *Emotional intelligence: Why it can matter more than IQ for character, health and lifelong achievement*. Bantam Books.

Hamann, S. (2001). Cognitive and neural mechanisms of emotional memory. *Trends in Cognitive Sciences*, 5(9), 394–400.

Immordino-Yang, M. H., & Damasio, A. (2007). We feel, therefore we learn: The relevance of affective and social neuroscience to education. *Mind, Brain, and Education*, 1(1), 3–10.

Izquierdo, I., Furini, C. R., & Myskiw, J. C. (2016). Fear memory. *Physiological Reviews*, 96(2), 695–750.

King, P. M., Magolda, M. B. B., & Massé, J. C. (2011). Maximizing learning from engaging across difference: The role of anxiety and meaning making. *Equity & Excellence in Education*, 44(4), 468–487.

LaBar, K. S. (2007). Beyond fear: Emotional memory mechanisms in the human brain. *Current Directions in Psychological Science*, 16(4), 173–177.

Li, L., Gow, A. D. I., & Zhou, J. (2020). The role of positive emotions in education: A neuroscience perspective. *Mind, Brain, and Education*, 14(3), 220–234.

Lujan, H. L., & DiCarlo, S. E. (2016). Humor promotes learning!. *Advances in Physiology Education*, 40(4), 433–434.

Moser, J. S., Schroder, H. S., Heeter, C., Moran, T. P., & Lee, Y. H. (2011). Mind your errors: Evidence for a neural mechanism linking growth mind-set to adaptive posterior adjustments. *Psychological science*, 22(12), 1484–1489.

Nolan, K., & Bergin, S. (2016). The role of anxiety when learning to program: A systematic review of the literature. https://mural.maynoothuniversity.ie/id/eprint/10306/1/SB-Role-2016.pdf.

Omar, S., Jain, J., & Noordin, F. (2013). Motivation in learning and happiness among the low science achievers of a Polytechnic Institution: An exploratory study. *Procedia-Social and Behavioral Sciences*, 90, 702–711.

Owens, M., Stevenson, J., Hadwin, J.A. and Norgate, R. (2014). When does anxiety help or hinder cognitive test performance? The role of working memory capacity. *British Journal of Psychology*, 105(1), pp. 92–101.

Pekrun, R., & Linnenbrink-Garcia, L. (Eds.) (2014) *Educational psychology handbook series. International handbook of emotions in education*. Routledge.

Raymond, J. (2009). Interactions of attention, emotion and motivation. *Progress in Brain Research*, 176, 293–308.

Salovey, P., & Mayer, J. D. (1990). Emotional intelligence. *Imagination, Cognition and Personality*, 9(3), 185–211.

Savage, B. M., Lujan, H. L., Thipparthi, R. R., & DiCarlo, S. E. (2017). Humor, laughter, learning, and health! A brief review. *Advances in Physiology Education*, 41(3), 341–347.

Schutz, P. A., & Pekrun, R. E. (2007). *Emotion in education*. Academic Press.

Serrat, O. (2017). *Knowledge solutions: Tools, methods, and approaches to drive organizational performance*. Springer.

Sommer, T., Gläscher, J., Moritz, S., & Büchel, C. (2008). Emotional enhancement effect of memory: Removing the influence of cognitive factors. *Learning & Memory*, 15(8), 569–573.

Tyng, C. M., Amin, H. U., Saad, M. N., & Malik, A. S. (2017). The influences of emotion on learning and memory. *Frontiers in Psychology*, 8, 1454.

Vedantam, S. (Host). (2021). Humor us [audio podcast episode]. https://hiddenbrain.org/podcast/humor-us/.

Vogel, S., & Schwabe, L. (2016). Learning and memory under stress: Implications for the classroom. *Science of Learning*, 1(1), 1–10.

Yeager, D. S., Hanselman, P., Walton, G. M., Murray, J. S., Crosnoe, R., Muller, C., & Dweck, C. S. (2019). A national experiment reveals where a growth mindset improves achievement. *Nature*, 573(7774), 364–369.

Yeager, D. S., Bryan, C. J., Gross, J. J., Murray, J. S., Krettek Cobb, D., HF Santos, P., & Jamieson, J. P. (2022). A synergistic mindsets intervention protects adolescents from stress. *Nature*, 607 (7919), 512–520.

Ziv, A. (2014). Using humor to develop creative thinking. In P. E. Mcghee (Ed.), *Humor and children's development* (pp. 99–116). Routledge.

Part V

Tying It All Together and Looking Ahead

12 Designing for Optimal Learning

I devote this chapter to more tactical adult learning principles. I begin by setting the record straight on several common learning myths that exist in the wild. I then shift to discuss Merrill's principles of instruction, how to manage the learning environment, the benefit of storytelling, and the tenets of the universal design for learning. However, before introducing the common learning myths in learning and development (L&D), I first establish the context of learning experience design (LXD).

This chapter centers on the idea that the professional designing for learning—whether it be a proper learning experience designer, instructional designer, program manager, teacher, coach, or anyone else with any other title—must know and apply the learning principles covered in this course at the right time and place, to do their job well. According to Jahnke et al. (2022), learning experience design is a hybrid discipline that relies on knowledge about learning and cognition, plus skills from user experience, instructional design, and technology. Further, Jahnke et al. (2022) stated that LXD consists of the following dimensions: social/sociocultural; technological; and pedagogical.

It is upon this conceptualization of LXD that this chapter is based. Therefore, as you read this chapter, please consider the various concepts from an LXD mindset: "As a learning experience designer, I want to understand the facts from the fiction, that I may ultimately know precisely how and when to apply the right principles, at the right time, for the right project."

Debunking Common L&D Myths

Myth 1: Learning Styles

One of the most enduring and prevailing myths in the learning world is that of *learning styles*. There are three key tenets identified in the literature relating to this seductive, pervasive idea (Hattie & O'Leary, 2025). First, the four common learning styles most frequently referenced are the visual, auditory, kinesthetic (i.e. hands-on), and read/write. Second, learners possess a particular aptitude or style in how they process information most effectively (e.g. "I learn best through images and diagrams"). Therefore, third, individuals learn best when the instruction matches their optimal learning style. However, while it is true that many learners express a preference for one style over another, often in a medium for which they believe to have an inherent strength (Riener & Willingham, 2010), as of 2025 there exists no scientific evidence that demonstrates that greater recall is achieved or that a learner performs better as a result of relying on one style over another (Kirschner, 2017; Pashler et al., 2008).

Scholars Hattie and O'Leary (2025) recently reviewed 17 distinct meta-analyses of learning style research. They concluded that the 17 meta-analyses captured and represented

DOI: 10.4324/9781003593607-17

two distinct types of studies: (1) those that measured the impact of matching a learner's preferred learning style with the instructional approach (i.e. effect size studies, *d*), and (2) those that evaluated the relationship between learner's learning style and achievement (i.e. correlation studies, *r*). In short, they found effect sizes close to zero for studies that explored matching one's preferred learning style with the instructional approach. And while they found higher correlations for achievement ($r = 0.24$), they admitted, however, that this still falls short of demonstrating *causation*. They further observed that much of the 2,500 studies that have been conducted on learning styles fall short of the necessary rigor and are characterized by incorrect statistical calculations, major confounding factors, low validity, and, frankly, give the impression of advocacy. Ultimately, therefore, they concluded that there is no evidence that a positive impact exists for matching learning styles to instructional styles.

Please understand the key distinction that exists between a learner's *preference* and their *ability*. While there is truth to the notion that prior experiences help someone adapt to similar circumstances (i.e. we rely on what we already know as our starting point to learn new concepts), the myth of learning styles goes one step too far by suggesting that a learner is necessarily wired to perform better when presented with their preferred medium. Instead, research consistently finds that most learners perform similarly to each other across different styles and mediums (Pashler et al., 2008). In sum, while a certain method or process *can* improve learning in a proper context, it is not a product of the way a learner's brain functions, per se. Rather, learning is enhanced as a result of the instruction that provides learners with the right tools and knowledge to meet performance expectations. Put another way, proper design, facilitation, and context lead to better learning, not a learner's "style."

Myth 2: Right, Left, and the Reptilian Brain

With the ever-increasing prevalence of physiological and neurological science in discussions and courses on adult learning, it may come as no surprise that its canonization has brought with it some unique myths that have found their way into prevalent adult learning texts over the years. Perhaps none have captured the imagination like that of the *left-* and *right-brained-ness*, and the related idea of the *triune brain*. The reason these two pseudoscientific ideas are related is that both share at their core a significant oversimplification of the inner structure of the brain that enables it to function at such a high level of performance, that is, through *lateralization*. As we discussed in Chapter 4, it is true that lateralized functions do exist in the brain, such as language being managed by two specialized parts of the left hemisphere. However, examples like these do not justify the notion that individual people are either "left-brain dominant" or "right-brain dominant." Instead, it is more accurate to think of the brain in this way: that all components and hemispheres of the brain work together in a complimentary fashion, which has been proven by neuroimaging (Goswami, 2004).

A related brain myth, the *triune brain* model, is an erroneous model of the brain that stems from Paul MacLean and his several decades-old publications on the subject. According to his work, there are three purported levels to the brain, increasing from the "simple" functions of (1) the *reptilian brain* (brainstem) managing instinct (breathing, motor function), (2) the limbic system or *mammalian brain* in charge of emotions, and (3) the *neomammalian brain* (neocortex) controlling the "complex" higher-order functions that are typically associated with humans, such as decision making and language.

However, this view of the brain implies strongly that humans are the outcome of the evolutionary process (i.e. descendants of ancient reptiles). But modern research has proven

this to be entirely false: our brains do not come from reptile origins (Cesario et al., 2020; Hain et al., 2022). It is true that the structures and functions of different organisms' nervous systems have simply changed and evolved many times over, some even resulting in brains being more structurally complex than humans (Cesario et al., 2020). However, to compare a reptile's brain to a human's is far more difficult than even apples to oranges. This is in part because a reptile's brain does not share the same structures, nor are any parts of our brain built on top of a supposed reptilian brain; they are, in fact, completely different systems that have their own unique evolutionary histories (Cesario et al., 2020). To be clear, the idea of shared or similar anatomies is something seen across much of the animal kingdom (Steffen et al., 2022). But as research has shown, this simply does not equate to humans and reptiles necessarily originating from the same species. That myth has safely been debunked.

Myth 3: The Learning Pyramid

Another prevalent myth in L&D is the *learning pyramid.* (A simple Google search will yield plenty of depictions.) It originates from Edgar Dale's *cone of learning*, which was a much simpler model that was meant to serve as a top-down descriptive model which organized instructional methods by increasing concreteness of the learning experience (Subramony et al., 2014). Over time however, percentages were eventually added to the various layers, making the model far more prescriptive in nature, and ordering the instructional methods described into a sort of hierarchy. These numbered attributions are a product of proliferation by the National Training Laboratories (Letrud, 2012; Masters, 2013), who claim to have researched the matter, though the data for that and other proclaimed sources for the numbers have never seen the light of day—especially not in peer reviewed journals—and the percentages themselves frequently change each time the pyramid resurfaces (Masters, 2013; Subramony et al., 2014). Despite the lack of an empirical basis and failure to stand up to scientific scrutiny, the pyramid somehow remains a frequent visual in popular science and even finds its way into scholarly articles (Masters, 2013). (If you do not believe me, simply take a look at LinkedIn for a few minutes.) Sadly, this proliferation is likely due to the pyramid's clean, intuitive presentation—meanwhile simultaneously reinforcing the dubious claim that certain instructional methods are inherently superior to others (Subramony et al., 2014).

Merrill's Principles of Instruction

With these three myths debunked, I now shift to more scientifically sound principles of learning. Whenever designing a training program, curriculum, or learning experience, it is important to begin with a strong foundation. A solid block in that foundation to consider applying is Dr. David Merrill's classic, *First Principles of Instruction* (Merrill, 2002). Dr. Merrill's work is a synthesis of the many commonalities existing between the different and evolving instructional theories that preceded it. Dr. Merrill's first principles of instruction include: problem-centered; activation; demonstration; application; integration. I unpack each principle next.

Problem-Centered

Merrill's (2002) initial principle of instruction asserts that learning is promoted when learners are engaged in *solving problems.* He considers a "problem" to be any activity that requires the learner to complete a whole task and not just one or two components of the

task. Merrill argued that learning is enhanced if the learners are initially shown the whole task they will be able to complete by the end of the learning experience (e.g. module or course), and further enhanced if "learners solve a progression of problems that are explicitly compared to one another" (Merrill, 2002, p. 45).

The science behind Merrill's first principle of instruction stems from the psychological concepts we discussed in Chapter 2. That is, expertise is optimally developed when *doing* is involved. Also, desirable difficulty is "desirable" because it requires a healthy level of challenge to complete. Lastly, please do not forget a critical neuroscientific principle: mistakes and errors are beneficial for our learning because (1) the resistance forces the brain to focus and work, both of which increase the plasticity that will occur as a result; and (2) the recognition of a mistake/error causes the brain to release acetylcholine, thus preparing the neurons to "learn" what to do differently so as to not repeat the mistake the next time. In total, problem-centered instruction is scientifically sound.

Activation

The second of Merrill's principles of instruction, shared by other popular methods, including Keller's ARCS motivation model (Keller, 1987) and the Katzell–Kirkpatrick evaluation model (Kirkpatrick & Kirkpatrick, 2016), is to *activate* the learner's mind by generating attention, relevance, and align new information with what is already known. Ideally, the first thing you as a designer hope to accomplish is to provide learners with the proper context to approach the learning, by answering the question of *why* the material is important and *what* learners need to understand beforehand to complete this training.

For this to occur, it is even more important to ensure the training is at a level the learners can understand and relate to (Merrill, 2002). Recall from previous chapters on social constructivism and expertise development that learners have a *zone of proximal development* where learning is most effective when the difficulty of the activity is just outside of their current capabilities and requires the assistance of a more knowledgeable other person before they can perform the task on their own. By finding that sweet spot between *undesirably easy* and *undesirably difficult*, while also conveying explicitly why this training is a valuable resource for your learners, they will be more likely to engage in the learning process and learn more from the experience as a direct result.

To illustrate, consider a basic 1-hour training at work. The facilitator might begin with an anecdote, story, joke, or something else to initially capture the participants' *attention*. But we know that in and of itself, that anecdote has a short-lived effect. Therefore, a layer of context highlighting the relevance of the training and its connection to their work, would further serve to "activate" the learners' minds. A relevant, well-placed story (as we will discuss later in the chapter), could have a particularly captivating effect. Then lastly, all throughout the training, relating each new concept to anything previously known by the learners would also increase the efficacy of the learning experience. In sum, capturing the learners' attention, establishing the relevance of the training, and relating the material to prior knowledge all serve to "activate" the learners' minds.

Demonstration

Merrill's (2002) next principle involves showing how the material relates to the expected learning outcomes and how things work in the real world, while never limiting instruction to just theoretical constructs. For a demonstration to be most effective, it must be (1) explicitly described and (2) situationally varied, while maintaining (3) overall consistency with the stated performance objectives. In this way, learners can gain a deeper understanding of the dynamics

of the process, while still having foundational knowledge to build upon in the field when things do not go as planned. Do you recall in Chapter 2, the flight demonstrations offered at the Navy Fighter Weapons School? The Top Gun students were first shown the intuition and techniques required to execute a specific maneuver in a certain situation; they then went out and practiced for several hours what they had been taught. Immediately following, the afternoons were spent reviewing their practice sessions. This highly successful pattern of developing elite fighter pilots all began with the daily *demonstration.*

Remember, learning is not merely about giving or presenting information. That may be a necessary step, but it is *never* sufficient. Learning is also a way of preparing learners to discover things on their own as well. In a similar vein, as a learning professional, you serve as a learner's guide, and your goal at this adult stage is to support learners in their efforts to read between the lines and see the deeper meaning of what they are learning, so they can increasingly understand the material now, and then continue their learning long after the training or learning experience has ended.

Application

The *application* principle builds on the foundation set during the activation stage, where now, instead of being guided by the instructor, learners start to tackle new and varied problems with diminishing levels of coaching, all while also starting to reflect on their performance and how they might improve. Additionally, it remains important to provide learners with situations that promote consistency in the approach that they are using to maintain focus on the desired performance outcomes. The key is that at this stage of the learning process, the level of responsibility shifts to the learner, as he/she aligns learned concepts with their own needs.

Integration

The final principle of Merrill's (2002) model involves reflection and active demonstration of new skills and knowledge to others. Similar to how an artist may show their latest work to their friends and colleagues, the purpose of this stage is to allow learners to appreciate how far they have progressed/learned since the learning experience started. After all, how can learners know what was gained from the learning process if their skills and abilities are the same as before? As a learning designer, developing opportunities for learners to "show off" by producing artifacts from the "journey" is critical to making the entire effort worthwhile both for the learners and yourself.

Managing the Environment

Facilitating In-person Learning

Historically, learning was once considered a *passive* exercise where the learner was little more than an observer passively receiving information from a central figure, often a single instructor, who dictated every aspect of the learning process. While this approach can still be meaningful when working with younger learners who benefit from the increased structure, professionals need to be able to confidently adapt and find success within rapidly shifting environments. Thus, effective training should also seek to improve the adaptive transfer of skills across various contexts and circumstances (Bell & Kozlowski, 2008).

Indeed, one of the most important shifts in learning science over the past hundred years is towards *active learning* design. This means giving learners ample opportunities to engage

with the material on a personal level where they can participate in the learning process (e.g. through trips, activities, and projects) rather than merely being a passive observer. Simultaneously, the instructor in this case also takes on a new role as a learning *facilitator*, where instead of prescribing a rigid roadmap with spoon-fed information for the learner to follow, they instead provide consistent feedback at every major milestone and steady guidance when necessary or explicitly asked for. Because this design approach is more open-ended, there is a greater need for having *contingent teaching strategies* (Luckin, 2008; van de Pol et al., 2010) in place, where instructors are able and willing to recognize when learners may need *more* or *less* guidance and/or scaffolding, to maximize their learning (van de Pol et al., 2010; Wood & Middleton, 1975).

Another shift in organizational training today is the rise of *informal learning*, which I discuss more in Chapter 13. However, informal learning is also critical to this topic, as organizational learning environments increasingly incorporate employees' supervisors and managers to provide on-the-job training and added context that relates to a learner's specific role and responsibilities in an organization (Macneil, 2001). Because of this, designers are also increasingly expected to design training programs for those in middle management so they can more effectively provide coaching and guidance on an as-needed basis outside of a formal training environment. These *train-the-trainer* programs often focus more on soft skills like leadership, communication, and facilitation. Another benefit of these programs relates to the design work itself, as incorporating these employees into the learning process offers much-needed insight and establishes a feedback loop between L&D staff and those working in other functional areas of the organization.

The actual process of facilitation varies depending on the circumstances and instructor preferences. That being said, the most consistent elements of learning facilitation are that learners have access to ample coaching, exemplary models of varying situations, and that any knowledge is immediately applicable to their everyday tasks, while any evaluations or activities conducted are authentic and measure performance relevant to the learner's organizational context (Choi & Hannafin, 1995).

Facilitating Remote Learning

Recall from Chapter 7 (the multimedia chapter) that, so far, no universally accepted theory of what constitutes effective e-learning currently exists, and many of the theories applied to remote learning were first designed and studied in the context of in-person learning. As a result, depending on how e-learning is defined, it can be imaged as an entirely separate practice that is in desperate need of a theoretical framework to justify a largely self-paced approach to learning, or instead, as an extension of traditional in-person instruction that uses technology to *enhance* rather than *replace* foundational approaches to learning (Dillenbourg et al., 2002). Also, by choosing to define e-learning as an extension of in-person learning, the gap shrinks between these two approaches and instead shifts the focus away from theoretical dogmas and places the emphasis on the challenges and exciting new dynamics that come with applying theories like behaviorism, social constructivism, and cognitive neuroscience in a virtual learning environment.

Since remote learning does share many similarities with in-person learning, it also requires many of the same considerations for design as were mentioned in the last section, albeit with their own caveats. For example, active learning also has a place in remote learning, though utilization often requires providing additional training on pertinent software applications that facilitate the active learning process. Resolving these deficiencies can be done in several different ways, including providing job aids or short video tutorials that demonstrate the basic user interface for learners, ideally without over-encumbering them

with more pedantic examples of its use. That said, by simply providing contingent learning strategies like these for your learners, who may or may not need them, you are already providing a more dynamic and responsive learning environment that can respond to the learners' needs as they arise while still benefiting from the accessibility that remote learning enables.

The second half of remote learning often overlooked in adult learning and organizational training initiatives is, as with in-person learning, *facilitation*. Before the advent of teleconferencing software made "face-to-face" and group meetings more accessible, the inaccessibility of real-time collaboration across the internet was a major obstacle to overcome, and many remote and e-learning solutions often lacked any form of collaboration beyond what was possible in a chat box. Today, with a variety of tools available that can make remote learning a more constructive and collaborative process, learning designers can do far better.

Facilitation of remote learning also brings unique challenges, not the least of which are maintaining student privacy, data security, and encouraging learner participation—all additional constraints for professionals to work around. Thankfully, many of the same tools relevant to in-person learning facilitation work in a remote learning environment. The key point here is that remote learning requires the same considerations as its in-person counterpart, and at the end of the day *sound application of learning science* is what matters most.

To be clear, remote learning (like all forms of learning) can be designed poorly, where the remoteness becomes an easy substitute for methods considered too costly, or worse, the learning process is entirely taken for granted. However, when designed with evidence-based principles in mind, remote learning can be an extremely effective and scalable option for learners today.

Storytelling

No other form of instruction or conveying information has prevailed over time like *storytelling*. The use of anecdotes, tales, and stories to illustrate concepts and communicate ideas, beliefs, and cultural norms well beyond the years of origin is probably the first example of a systematic approach to instruction in our collective history (Bruner, 1987; Bettelheim, 2010). Make no mistake: storytelling is a unique skill and talent, and significantly impacts the way individuals construct meaning out of the world. Unsurprisingly, the innate magnetism of storytelling continues to be an integral part of training, as it provides a natural scaffolding upon which designers can organize the learning journey, while also providing learners with a narrative structure they can follow. In this way, a well-designed scenario or story can establish clear lines of cause and effect, while also providing additional context into someone else's thinking in such a way that is difficult to do by any other instructional means (Bruner, 1991, 2009).

The notion that stories play an important part in organizations is hardly groundbreaking. Fundamentally, storytelling is a *dialogical, divergent, emergent*, and *collaborative* process (Abma, 2003). For our purposes, let us simplify that to a social constructivist process (Boyce, 1995), as stories are a powerful medium in which to influence a learner's way of thinking and their feelings towards things such as change within the organization. In short, stories are very effective tools to help change behavior because stories impact our brain chemistry. So what exactly is happening when we hear a story?

When a story catches one's attention there is a small release of cortisol, and the story hearer begins caring about what is happening. We also empathize with the characters—a process referred to as "transportation." Specifically, oxytocin is the neurochemical responsible for empathy and narrative transportation. According to research by Zak (2013, 2015), the production of oxytocin in the brain leads to increased levels of trustworthiness,

generosity, charity, and compassion among individuals. Oxytocin also enhances our sensitivity to social cues. Dr. Zak stated:

> It seems that once we are attentive and emotionally engaged, our brains go into mimic mode and mirror the behaviors that the characters in the story are doing, or might do. As social creatures we are biased toward engaging with others, and effective stories motivate us to help others.
>
> (Zak, 2015, para. 32)

The oxytocin that is released during storytelling creates a brain connection between the storyteller and the listener. This connection from oxytocin release is triggered by mirror neurons, in a process called *neural coupling* (Ariel, n.d.). The storyteller's and story hearer's brains are synchronized, as the listener's brain fires the same patterns of the speaker's brain. When we engage in a story (even if its fictional), what happens neurologically seems "real" in our brains and bodies. For example, think of a time when someone described a delicious meal, causing the listener's mouth to salivate in response. It is a similar phenomenon. Although fictional stories are just imaginary, our bodies tend to physically respond to them as if they were real.

Now if a story describes an emotionally-charged event, or for a particularly engaging story, the brain also releases dopamine. Stories with intense situations have the potential to elevate dopamine levels, which we learned in Chapter 4 helps with learner focus, motivation, and memory. Our brain's reward center also releases dopamine when a story has a happy ending or if it imparts a life lesson. Research has shown that dopamine serves to help the listener find meaning in the story's message, which contributes to long-lasting retention (Ashrof, 2021). So to be crystal clear, stories affect behaviors. In fact, several studies have discovered that stories can be far more persuasive than facts. If a story captures the listener's attention, it can evoke powerful responses, which in turn can translate into concrete action (FoST, n.d.).

When considering how to leverage storytelling in a training program, an important question to ask as designers is: *What makes for a good story?* Answering that question can be difficult, but evidence and history suggest that Freytag's pyramid (also known now as a *dramatic arc*) can be particularly effective: exposition, rising action, climax, falling action, and denouement/resolution (Freytag, 2008 [1863]).

Additionally, most compelling stories share common themes including contrasting or disparate emotional themes (e.g. good to bad, or bad to good), a causal link that ties events together, some element of the story that relates to the reader, or extraordinary circumstances which stand out from ordinary life (Taylor et al., 2002). Increasing the tension in the story during the rising action and climax helps to keep the audience's attention (Zak, 2015). This triggers our natural negativity bias (i.e. the tendency to focus on bad, threatening things). We are afraid that whatever happens in the story could happen to us, and we need to learn how to deal with these potential dangers. As stated earlier, when our brain maintains attention, it releases stress hormones, and our focus is high.

In organizations specifically, stories serve as focal points that create a shared social reality (Boyce, 1995) for everyone privy to or otherwise attached to the story. Such stories are often the bedrock of an organization's culture and its socialization processes, which serve to sustain the teams, departments, and other functional aspects of the organization's operation. A handy list of how stories come to impact organizational function and structure can be found below (Boyce, 1996):

- Expressing the organizational experience of members or clients.
- Confirming the shared experiences and shared meaning of organizational members and groups within the organization.

- Orienting and socializing new organizational members.
- Amending and altering the organizational reality.
- Developing, sharpening, and renewing the sense of purpose held by organizational members.
- Preparing a group (or groups) for planning, implementing plans and decision-making in line with shared purposes.
- Co-creating vision and strategy.

The fact that storytelling is an innate human trait that is both important to individuals and the groups to which they belong means that professionals, particularly in organizations, should also incorporate storytelling elements that fall within the confines of the culture and socialization process that the learners exist within. For multiple reasons, stories provide structure, they create emotional connection, and they help us put change into perspective. Storytelling functions as a reflective process—it can push us out of familiar ways of thinking and facilitates the reexamination of ourselves in a new light.

Universal Design for Learning

As professionals, it is a sin to over-emphasize the "typical" learner. That is, an expert professional knows that *all learners* should be considered, at all times, in the design process. Adult learning demands that we approach our instructional projects with an eye toward a greater level of diversity, and therefore requires that our learning activities, materials, assessments, etc. remain accessible and effective for a spectrum of potential learners. In this manner, we want to approach our work with "universal" accessibility and applicability. Originating in architectural design through the pioneering work of Ron Mace, ***universal design*** is an approach that seeks to develop systems, environments, and processes that are more accommodating for *everyone* who uses them. Indeed, one curious outcome of using universal design is something referred to as the *curb-cut effect* (Zeff, 2007). This effect refers to the unintended benefits that came from when municipalities started designing sidewalks and building entryways using ramps instead of steps to make public spaces more accessible to wheelchair users, which resulted in many other people benefitting from the increased ease of use as well, including those riding bikes, pushing baby strollers, and anyone shuffling around heavy cargo on the street (Zeff, 2007). The takeaway here is that while universal design may have at its core the intent to make our world more accessible to those of us with differences or disabilities, it often has the added benefit of making the world more accessible *for everyone*.

The importance of universal design in adult learning is most evident when looking at the development of learning assessments, where commonly used pen-and-paper testing protocols frequently put many different kinds of learners, able-bodied or otherwise, at a disadvantage (Rose, 2000). Even more damning, many traditional assessments measure learning outcomes in isolation from the context (tools, processes, and people) around which they perform those functions, bringing into question what value evaluation provides if it fails to measure real-world performance. In addition, many tests and assessments are designed in a way that passing assessments becomes the ultimate achievement or hurdle to overcome. Together, these transform the evaluation process from a positive one that can provide invaluable feedback to a learner into something that promotes stress and redirects focus away from where it is most needed: the learning process (Rose, 2000).

To overcome these challenges, designers should provide real-world, simulated, or on-the-job evaluations that measure performance where it will occur but in a way that also provides alternate means for engagement whenever possible. For example, someone with

dyslexia will likely struggle with a pen-and-paper exam, but they may be more than capable of expressing their understanding verbally or demonstratively (Rose, 2000). Providing alternative means for evaluation like this is not unfair as long as every learner is afforded an opportunity to participate in these methods. Remember: universal design is about making processes more equitable for *everyone*.

It is also worth pointing out that many neurodivergent traits are not visibly apparent, and just because someone looks like they do not need accommodations does not make that true. (When all else fails, one might consider asking politely if there are any considerations for the learning experience that might make for more optimal learning for that person.) Also, other conditions including testing anxiety can be particularly challenging for learning designers to overcome, as evaluation and feedback are critical to supporting a learner's growth and continued success. In those particular situations, it may be worth making an effort to motivate learners past their anxiety and ensure that learners never feel like the process is final. After all, we know that a well-designed learning program uses mistakes as powerful tools for learning, and for learners to understand that, you, as the designer, must provide opportunities for remediation so that failure is always understood to be a natural and temporary stage in the learning process—not something to be feared.

To help you better understand how you can incorporate principles of universal design into your work, researchers at the University of Connecticut developed a formidable list of the many ways that instruction can be more accessible to a wider variety of learners with different backgrounds, abilities, and limitations. You can find the entire list of design principles below (McGuire et al., 2003), and please consider referencing this list frequently, as with time and practice, many of these will become second nature:

- **Equitable use:** Instruction is designed to be useful to and accessible to people with diverse abilities. Provide the same means of use for all students, identical whenever possible, and equivalent when not.
- **Flexibility in use:** Instruction is designed to accommodate a wide range of individual abilities. Provide choice in methods of use.
- **Simple and intuitive instruction:** Instruction is designed in a straightforward and predictable manner, regardless of the student's experience, knowledge, language skills, or current concentration level. Eliminate unnecessary complexity.
- **Perceptible information:** Instruction is designed so that necessary information is communicated effectively, regardless of ambient conditions or the student's sensory abilities.
- **Tolerance for error:** Instruction anticipates variation in individual student learning pace and prerequisite skills.
- **Low physical effort:** Instruction is designed to minimize nonessential physical effort in order to allow maximum attention to learning.
- **Size and space for approach and use:** Instruction is designed with consideration for appropriate size and space for approach, reach, manipulations, and use regardless of a student's body size, posture, mobility, and communication needs.
- **A community of learners:** The instructional environment promotes interaction and communication among students and between students and faculty.
- **Instructional climate:** Instruction is designed to be welcoming and inclusive. High expectations are espoused for all students.

References

Abma, T. A. (2003). Learning by telling: Storytelling workshops as an organizational learning intervention. *Management Learning*, 34(2), 221–240.

Ariel. (n.d.). Why storytelling works: The science. www.arielgroup.com/why-storytelling-works-the-science/#:~:text=When%20the%20brain%20sees%20or,is%20known%20as%20neural%20coupling.

Ashrof, V. (2021). Storytelling: A scientific analysis. https://countercurrents.org/2021/05/storytelling-a-scientific-analysis.

Bell, B. S., & Kozlowski, S. W. J. (2008). Active learning: Effects of core training design elements on self-regulatory processes, learning, and adaptability. *Journal of Applied Psychology*, 93, 296–316.

Bettelheim, B. (2010). *The uses of enchantment: The meaning and importance of fairy tales.* Vintage.

Boyce, M. E. (1995). Collective centring and collective sense-making in the stories and storytelling of one organization. *Organization Studies*, 16(1), 107–137.

Boyce, M. E. (1996) Organizational story and storytelling: A critical review, *Journal of Organizational Change Management* 9(5): 5–26.

Bruner, J. (1987). Life as narrative. *Social Research*, 54(1), 11–32.

Bruner, J. (1991). The narrative construction of reality. *Critical Inquiry*, 18(1), 1–21.

Bruner, J. S. (2009). *Actual minds, possible worlds.* Harvard University Press.

Cesario, J., Johnson, D. J., & Eisthen, H. L. (2020). Your brain is not an onion with a tiny reptile inside. *Current Directions in Psychological Science*, 29(3), 255–260.

Choi, J. I., & Hannafin, M. (1995). Situated cognition and learning environments: Roles, structures, and implications for design. *Educational Technology Research and Development*, 43(2), 53–69.

Dillenbourg, P., Schneider, D., & Synteta, P. (2002). Virtual learning environments. https://telearn.hal.science/file/index/docid/190701/filename/Dillernbourg-Pierre-2002a.pdf.

FoST. (n.d.). Paul Zak: Empathy, neurochemistry, and the dramatic arc. Retrieved from https://futureofstorytelling.org/case-study/paul-zak-empathy-neurochemistry-and-the-dramatic-arc.

Freytag, G. (2008 [1863]). *Freytag's technique of the drama: An exposition of dramatic composition and art*, trans. E. J. MacEwan. Scott, Foresman and Company.

Goswami, U. (2004). Neuroscience and education. *British Journal of Educational Psychology*, 74(1), 1–14.

Hain, D., Gallego-Flores, T., Klinkmann, M., Macias, A., Ciirdaeva, E., Arends, A., ... & Laurent, G. (2022). Molecular diversity and evolution of neuron types in the amniote brain. *Science*, 377 (6610), eabp8202.

Hattie, J., & O'Leary, T. (2025). Learning styles, preferences, or strategies? An explanation for the resurgence of styles across many meta-analyses. *Educational Psychology Review*, 37(2), 1–26.

Jahnke, I., Schmidt, M., Earnshaw, Y., & Tawfik, A. A. (2022). Theoretical considerations of learning experience design. In H. Leary, S. P. Greenhalgh, K. B. Staudt Willet, & M. H. Cho (Eds.), *Theories to influence the future of learning design and technology.* EdTech Books.

Keller, J. M. (1987). Development and use of the ARCS model of instructional design. *Journal of Instructional Development*, 10(3), 2–10.

Kirkpatrick, J. D., & Kirkpatrick, W. K. (2016). *Kirkpatrick's four levels of training evaluation.* Association for Talent Development.

Kirschner, P. A. (2017). Stop propagating the learning styles myth. *Computers & Education*, 106, 166–171.

Letrud, K. (2012). A rebuttal of NTL Institute's learning pyramid. *Education*, 133(1), 117–124.

Luckin, R. (2008). The learner centric ecology of resources: A framework for using technology to scaffold learning. *Computers & Education*, 50(2), 449–462.

Macneil, C. (2001). The supervisor as a facilitator of informal learning in work teams. *Journal of Workplace Learning*, 13(6), 246–253.

Masters, K. (2013). Edgar Dale's pyramid of learning in medical education: A literature review. *Medical Teacher*, 35(11), e1584–e1593.

McGuire, J. M., Scott, S. S., & Shaw, S. F. (2003). Universal design for instruction: The paradigm, its principles, and products for enhancing instructional access. *Journal of Postsecondary Education and Disability*, 17(1), 11–21.

Merrill, M. D. (2002). First principles of instruction. *Educational Technology Research and Development*, 50, 43–59.

Pashler, H., McDaniel, M., Rohrer, D., & Bjork, R. (2008). Learning styles: Concepts and evidence. *Psychological Science in the Public Interest*, 9(3), 105–119.

Riener, C., & Willingham, D. (2010). The myth of learning styles. *Change: The Magazine of Higher Learning*, 42(5), 32–35.

Rose, D. (2000). Universal design for learning. *Journal of Special Education Technology*, 15(4), 47–51.

Steffen, P. R., Hedges, D., & Matheson, R. (2022). The brain is adaptive not triune: How the brain responds to threat, challenge, and change. *Frontiers in Psychiatry*, 13, 802606.

Subramony, D. P., Molenda, M., Betrus, A. K., & Thalheimer, W. (2014). The mythical retention chart and the corruption of Dale's cone of experience. *Educational Technology*, 54(6), 6–16.

Taylor, S. S., Fisher, D., & Dufresne, R. L. (2002). The aesthetics of management storytelling: A key to organizational learning. *Management Learning*, 33(3), 313–330.

van de Pol, J., Volman, M., & Beishuizen, J. (2010). Scaffolding in teacher–student interaction: A decade of research. *Educational Psychology Review*, 22, 271–296.

Wood, D., & Middleton, D. (1975). A study of assisted problem-solving. *British Journal of Psychology*, 66(2), 181–191.

Zak, P. (2013). How stories change the brain. https://greatergood.berkeley.edu/article/item/how_stories_change_brain.

Zak, P. (2015). Why inspiring stories make us react: The neuroscience of narrative. *Cerebrum*, 2, 2.

Zeff, R. (2007). Universal design across the curriculum. *New Directions for Higher Education*, 137, 27–44.

13 Current and Near-Future Trends

Informal Learning

The classic 70–20–10 heuristic of employee development maintains that approximately 70% of individual learning and development occurs through relevant but challenging experiences, 20% through relationships and social interactions, and only 10% through formal learning activities (Center for Creative Leadership, 2020; Watkins et al., 2014). Note that this is a common heuristic, but by no means is it actually research supported. Remember, from what we learned about several myths in Chapter 12, a heuristic or model does not necessarily equate to being factual or research supported. In my experience, however, the 70-20-10 heuristic is not far from reality.

So with roughly 10% of individual workplace learning occurring through formal channels, this means that about 90% occurs through informal means. Martinez and Whiting characterized *informal learning* in this way:

> Informal learning can be defined as the pursuit of any knowledge, skill, or understanding that occurs outside a formal or non-formal learning event, such as a classroom, training facility, or eLearning course … Informal learning includes family discussions at home, Googling a topic on the Internet, seeking advice from a colleague, visits to museums, and other everyday experiences …
>
> (Martinez & Whiting, 2020)

In this manner, informal learning is essentially everything learned outside of the formal training/class environment. In workplace settings, recall from earlier in the book that this includes communities of practice, water cooler conversations, chat rooms (e.g. Slack), your team's or organization's intranet, conversations over coffee or lunch, etc.

The data are clear that since the pandemic of COVID-19, the workplace has seen a significant rise in employee participation in informal learning (Yan & Fan, 2022; Watkins & Marsick, 2021; OECD, 2021). So, what might have recently once been a 90% prevalence, informal learning in the workplace might now be 93%, 94%, or perhaps 95%. Therefore, it has never been more critical that professionals leverage this trend in their practice than now. But how? According to Martinez and Whiting (2020), there are four effective ways to design for optimal informal learning: (1) provide options for the learner; (2) design for collaboration, idea sharing, and peer interaction (i.e. design social learning experiences); (3) leverage the benefits of constructionism and project-based learning; and (4) leverage the benefits of gamification and playful competition.

First, provide learners *a choice* in their learning. In a workplace environment, professionals can provide learners a list of possible related topics, and only require mastery of one. You may also consider providing a library of resources in various media such as text, image,

DOI: 10.4324/9781003593607-18

audio (podcast), video, self-guided modules, and then allow learners to decide how to gain mastery of the topic. Also consider presenting any information in a non-linear way; instead, allow them to choose the order of topics they may want to learn first. Or, instead of a bulleted list or outline in a computer module, consider a more visual layout where they can choose the order from multiple topics.

Second, design to take advantage of *collaboration, idea sharing*, and *peer interaction*. While teamwork, collaboration, and group projects are all components of formal learning, informal learning is also well suited to benefit from social interaction. Bandura and Walters (1977) argued that "most human behavior is learned observationally through modeling: from observing others, one forms an idea of how new behaviors are performed, and on later occasions this coded information serves as a guide for action" (p. 22). Further, Lev Vygotsky (1978) maintained that social learning consists of learning through social interaction.

When more specific knowledge is needed by an individual, a personalized informal experience in the form of coaching or mentoring will allow a novice to learn directly from an expert. A learning experience that centers on group work and peer interaction will invite informal learning to take place as individuals pose questions to and receive answers from their teammates and colleagues. To do this, consider assigning group tasks or projects, or posing problems that require multiple individuals to complete. A technique to take advantage of the unscheduled nature of informal social learning is to design a wiki or forum system that leverages the knowledge of the community in a socially constructed manner. Lastly, an emerging trend in informal learning is *microlearning*—small learning units such as text phrases, photos, or audio snippets—and its associated affordances for instructional designers (Giurgiu, 2017). For the specific principles of microlearning design, see Zhang and West (2020).

Third, consider leveraging the benefits of *constructionism* and *project-based learning*. With constructionism and project-based learning, learners typically become active participants in the experience and learn organically as they work through a challenge. Designers working to implement informal learning principles can include opportunities for exploration and creation. Many organizations have implemented "innovation centers" or "creativity labs" where new ideas can be tested and prototyped. For example, Pixar fosters innovation and encourages their employees to develop new skills through their Pixar University. As part of the "university," employees can sign up for free classes in painting, ballet, or sculpting. Additionally, Lowe's Home Improvement company has created innovation labs where employees reimagine how to help customers using augmented reality to plan virtual home renovation projects. Allowing learning through experimentation and failure can lead to better quality products and services.

Last fourth, leverage the benefits of *gamification* and *playful competition*. Playful competition and gaming are proven mechanisms for increasing learner engagement (Steinkuehler & Squire, 2014). While the principle holds for formal learning, it is particularly effective in designing informal learning environments. Gamification is "a relatively recent term that describes using game thinking and game mechanisms in nongame contexts to engage users" (Steinkuehler & Squire, 2014, p. 389). The key criteria for an effective gamified design are exploration, immersion, socialization, and competition.

To design for exploration, it is important to design an experience that does not necessarily have a single path toward a solution. This allows the learners to truly discover, explore, make mistakes, and iterate. To design for immersion, it is important that the challenge be such that the only way to solve the problem is with dedicated, focused time, over an extended period. For example, learners can (a) build or produce an artifact from scratch, (b) solve a problem that requires the synthesis and application of multiple concepts

simultaneously, (c) give or receive feedback to or from peers or experts where they must refine their work as part of the final solution, or (d) some combination of all three. To design for competition, it is helpful to consider something that determines one or multiple winners. Challenges with levels, simulations, scoring, badges, and leaderboards are features of competition that you can incorporate into your design.

Organizations should provide governance and structure to the knowledge base that is possessed by the people that comprise the organization. Additionally, organizations should catalog the knowledge base, and provide a repository of information for all to benefit from. In accounting for these two things, the organization will be creating the framework for strong informal learning practices.

Performance Support Systems

A *performance support system* is any tool or system that allows an individual to learn while being systematically integrated with work. For example, a basic job aid is simply one (analog) form of performance support because it allows the user to perform the required task with minimal interruption. In this manner, learning via a performance support tool/system is often referred to as "learning in the flow of work" or "workflow learning." To be clear, workflow learning is a type of performance support; a person can receive performance support without necessarily learning, per se. Building on these ideas, we refer to any system of performance support that requires technology as an *electronic performance support system* (EPSS). EPSSs show promise for improving performance, but they are an evolving technology and the systems require continuous refinement to consistently produce quality results.

Virtual Reality

Compared to other educational technologies, *virtual reality* (VR) is a rather eclectic term that can refer to a variety of devices with a range of capabilities. However, for the sake of clarity and discussion, the scope of this section relates exclusively to the use of virtual reality headsets that track a user's movements and utilize haptic controllers that enable tactile interaction within the virtual environment such as Meta Platforms' *Meta Quest* line of products or Valve Corporation's *Index*.

Often priced at several hundred dollars for an entry-level product, these headsets have become an enticing value proposition for many organizations looking for ways to train their employees in environments that, while simulated, provide the opportunity to practice and apply relevant knowledge and skills in a more contextual or analogous setting to the real circumstances they will perform within. In addition, virtual reality enables employees to learn and practice skills in simulated environments that would otherwise be infeasible, impractical, or otherwise too dangerous to attempt in a real-world training scenario (Adamovich et al., 2009; Kaplan et al., 2021). In this way, simulated practice can provide a more authentic training experience than what may be currently possible via direct instruction, mentorship, or remote learning solutions.

The psychological reason virtual reality works is thanks to the concept of *embodiment*, which refers to our sense of individual will or agency, physical location in space, and personal ownership of self (Kilteni et al., 2012). This idea is especially relevant in this case as the virtual environment needs to provide an authentic feeling experience for users to suspend their disbelief and envision themselves as existing within the virtual space. In other words, if the virtual world feels too fake, users are far less likely to take the experience seriously or to behave authentically. Providing embodiment to users can be achieved in several different ways, including (Kilteni et al., 2012):

- **Location:** Having users interact with the environment from a first-person perspective as they do in real life and making it consistent with the real world.
- **Agency:** Enabling users to pick up, move, or otherwise use objects in the virtual space and by having the environment respond to their actions in turn.
- **Ownership:** Having the virtual body, or avatar, appear human-like so users can self-identify with their new body and by enabling user customization.

Virtual reality is also not limited to only one user at a time. Some of the greatest benefits of using virtual reality in organizations could be that multiple people, learners and trainers, can occupy the same virtual space simultaneously, irrespective of their location in the real world. This can allow trainers to facilitate in real time as learners progress through the virtual learning experience while also enabling facilitators to change the parameters of the environment in ways that would be impossible to do in any other format. However, note that virtual training is most often designed as a singular experience for an individual learner, though the potential is still there for collaborative learning, and that many of these benefits are not unique to virtual reality but possible through traditional methods as well (Bharwaney et al., 2022).

In addition, virtual reality enables real-time data analytics that can measure multiple dimensions of a learner's performance ranging from speed and accuracy to attention and focus. Based on this data, virtual environments have the unique advantage of being able to dynamically adapt to a learner's performance, either providing more or less guidance and support (Adamovich et al., 2009) while also progressing predictably so learners receive a consistent experience across various repetitions, further reinforcing their learning.

The current organizational landscape shows virtual reality finding a foothold in many high-value, high-risk sectors, including healthcare (Adamovich et al., 2009; Aïm et al., 2016; Nagendran et al., 2013), aviation (Abate et al., 2009), and engineering (Gavish et al., 2013; Wang et al., 2018), where the costs of purchasing and training learners with virtual reality devices is significantly less than what the consequences are if that learner were to make a fatal error in the field. It is also worth noting that many of the costs associated with virtual reality are front-loaded since these devices are reusable, and the virtual environments themselves are easy to adjust to different parameters, thereby allowing for the training of employees on various skills and in different environments simply by updating the simulations to fulfill entirely new training needs as they arise (Gavish et al., 2013).

With that said, virtual reality does come with some caveats. Chief among them is the *current* lack of a well-developed empirical foundation that supports virtual reality as being better than more traditional methods of instruction (Gavish et al., 2013). This issue is complicated further by the diversity of different devices and several studies that only compare learning outcomes against control groups that do not receive any form of alternative training at all (Grantcharov et al., 2004; Nagendran et al., 2013; Seymour et al., 2002), or otherwise suffering from small sample sizes (Seymour et al., 2002).

The actual process of developing virtual learning environments is another major hurdle for the widespread adoption of these devices, as learning and development professionals must either outsource their production to programmers, animators, and environmental designers with the expertise to translate learning designs into a virtual space or take on the immense challenge of learning these skills themselves. Currently, many companies that provide these services utilize generic assets (models, animations, lighting, user interfaces) available for purchase from freelance designers and curated in online stores hosted by the engine developers themselves, such as the Unity Asset Store and Unreal Engine Marketplace. While using these assets makes the design process more economical, learning designers are limited to whatever is available and may not find the necessary resources to

develop virtual environments that meet their organization's training needs. In addition, these assets vary considerably in style and quality, which can interfere with the embodiment process or result in bloated programs that modern virtual reality headsets may struggle to run at the necessary FPS (frames-per-second) to prevent feelings of motion sickness. As with many training constraints, these issues are solvable with ever-greater financial investments, while more off-the-shelf training solutions are always in development (Bharwaney et al., 2022). But ultimately, the increased investment will need to be weighed against the cost of producing more traditional forms of instruction.

One issue that is not immediately resolvable is how a considerable number of learners report being uncomfortable with using virtual reality headsets (Gavish et al., 2013), with some experiencing motion sickness, feelings of vertigo or claustrophobia, neck strain, and the inherent difficulty that comes from using visual aids such as glasses with these types of apparatus.

Altogether, this suggests that virtual reality will likely not replace traditional methods of instruction (Bharwaney et al., 2022). However, it does support the notion that virtual reality may still be useful in those instances where traditional experiential methods cannot be employed and that learners are likely to come away from the simulated experience with comparable levels of understanding (Kaplan et al., 2021). At its finest, virtual reality promises the best of both worlds: the convenience, safety, analytics, and scalability of remote learning while still providing an authentic training experience within an appropriate context and support structure that simulates the kinds of environments that learners will perform within.

Artificial Intelligence

At the time of this writing, artificial intelligence has only started to become an accessible and mainstream tool that organizations and their employees can utilize on an everyday basis. With the rapid adoption of OpenAI's ChaptGPT and similar large language models being integrated into seemingly every type of software available, there is no doubt AI will have an immense and lasting impact on training and development as well as how we, collectively as humans, live our professional lives.

These large language models (LLM) are a form of computationally modeled neural networks that are capable of recognizing and relating enormous patterns of data through an iterative computational process of *encoding* and *decoding* that gradually enables relevant swaths of data to become associated with one another as the model's parameters continue to tighten and refine its "understanding" (Amazon Web Services, n.d.). Also, many artificial intelligences like ChaptGPT and its derivatives incorporate sampled human feedback from previous questions and answers into the data sets to improve the accuracy and "mannerisms" of the artificial intelligence and make it more human-like in the way it responds to a user's questions and prompts (Stiennon et al., 2020).

Consider you are asked to fill in the blank for this sentence: "Toto, I've a feeling we're not in ______ anymore." If you've seen the 1939 film of *The Wizard of Oz*, the name of Dorothy's dog Toto and the phrasing of the sentence allowed your brain to make the association between the film's plot and Judy Garland's famous line. Large language models do much the same thing. However, unlike humans, they complete this process at an incredible rate and can consolidate tremendous amounts of information at a time (recall *bounded rationality*). What they cannot do is understand or create context (Baidoo-Anu & Ansah, 2023); as a result, an artificial intelligence like ChatGPT often provides odd, biased, or factually inaccurate responses if they have not been trained *extensively* (billions of times) on exact patterns of data. So, while artificial intelligence can answer the sample question, it

does so differently, instead relying on inserting the correct answer based on statistical and probabilistic likelihoods based on the sequence of words, not because it likes or understands films.

Based on the speed that artificial intelligence can process information and recognize patterns, it may not be surprising that its most productive use so far is as a knowledge-gathering tool where it is gradually replacing the traditional web search with dialogical results that consolidates data from multiple sources into a more comprehensive response more appropriate to a user's specific inquiry. In this way, artificial intelligence is not accomplishing anything so extreme as replacing how people think, work, or create. Rather, it helps to expedite one of the most time-consuming aspects of those tasks, which is collecting basic factual information and generalizing some preliminary inferences from that process.

The other use of artificial intelligence relevant to learning and development is the concept of adaptive learning. Defined as the use of machine learning algorithms and artificial intelligence to develop *custom learning solutions that can adapt to a learner's unique needs* (Wang et al., 2020), these systems are just now becoming possible thanks in large part to *incorporating more human feedback into artificial intelligence*, such as ChatGPT, through initiatives such as OpenAI's "GPTs" program (implemented in 2023). Put another way, artificial intelligence is only able to teach humans *after* learning from them.

In the context of adult learning, adaptive learning means that artificial intelligence can collect performance data from a learner, measure it against desired parameters, and suggest—if not outright design—customized learning paths that can address any shortcomings without training them on the material they already have familiarity with. Another, perhaps more benevolent approach, may involve using standardized tests where a learner's unique strengths, interests, and personal demographics are collected and processed by an artificial intelligence to build personalized development plans that align with organizational needs and the long-term career goals of employees. In either case, artificial intelligence offers an opportunity to build instruction around the learners, instead of expecting them to contort around the instruction, which is not only good news for learning outcomes as individualized instruction, including computer-based, is not only effective (Ma et al., 2014; Shute & Towle, 2003), but it also provides for a more equitable learning experience overall (Wang et al., 2020).

In the future, the unique ability of artificial intelligence to "learn" from its users will also enable organizations to take the groundwork of a system like ChatGPT and further refine it for their needs by establishing massive feedback loops between groups of employees, customers, and a centralized artificial intelligence; thereby increasing its accuracy and adaptability through ever larger sets of data, all without interfering with daily operations. Related to this idea is the rapidly growing market for entrepreneurial professionals to sell their trained systems through marketplaces curated by the developers, which may provide for more off-the-shelf solutions where the artificial intelligence is already pre-trained for a specific set of circumstances. In a sense, these will operate as places where individuals or organizations can shop for artificial employees or subject matter experts to meet their exact needs for a particular role.

However, it is necessary to remember that *artificial intelligence does not think*, nor should anyone put blind faith in its results. As a professional, a critical eye with a pinch of skepticism are in order. These technologies are only in their infancy and will require several years of research and refinement before they are precise enough to put significant faith into their use beyond basic, non-critical tasks. And even then, artificial intelligence will always require a human to supervise its use and ensure that results remain fair, unbiased, and true. In fact, many of the dangers that artificial intelligence presents are not a result of the

technology itself but rather from how people choose to use it. As an example, students and learners have already adopted systems like ChatGPT to write their essays, conduct research, and propose projects, where even a minor rewrite from the student can significantly reduce the ability to computationally detect whether the result is a product of artificial intelligence or a human (Tlili et al., 2023). This presents serious ethical concerns with regard to determining who "owns" the information an artificial intelligence outputs, whether it's the original authors, the developers who trained the AI, or the user who inserts the prompt. Therefore, focusing on sources of information that are both (1) original and (2) reputable is key for professional work. One sound technique is to seek peer-reviewed sources and work from scholars.

With Pandora's box opened and artificial intelligence being here to stay, learning professionals need to adjust how they design, implement, and assess their training projects and reevaluate how they support learners. Regardless of anything else, one guarantee is that your learners will use these technologies wherever possible. That is something that our profession must accept at this point.

That said, there are several things that artificial intelligence cannot do and require a human's innate abilities to accomplish; those are the knowledge and skills that forward-thinking learning designers will concentrate on from now on. First, emphasize the importance of learners being able to infer valuable insights from new information. Since artificial intelligence does not think, it fails to provide accurate responses involving circumstances it is not familiar with. Humans, on the other hand, are naturally talented and adaptive problem solvers who can synthesize new knowledge from their experiences and infer novel insights from the ecological conditions surrounding them. As such, project and problem-based learning activities that do not have pre-defined or singular solutions or that present moral and ethical challenges still require learners to engage with the material to produce well-thought-out solutions.

In addition, artificial intelligence is not particularly artistic since it lacks an imagination (Baidoo-Anu & Ansah, 2023), therefore, engaging learners in a creative, problem-solving process where they have to create something relevant based on what they have learned, will not only be rewarding but it is difficult for artificial intelligence to replicate that authentically. And finally, artificial intelligence can never replace flesh and blood. As such, any in-person or on-the-job training, by default, requires the practice of knowledge and skills in a real environment that artificial intelligence holds no sway over.

So, instead of trying to fight against the tide, consider this an opportunity to evolve and embrace artificial intelligence as another tool that learners can use to be successful. At the same time, ensure that your learning process continues to follow the evidence-based practices discussed in this book, and that every opportunity is used to connect the instructional process with your learners' individual needs, motivations, and performance requirements. If you can do that, artificial intelligence should not be a threat but rather an advantage to your work, your learners' work, and to the organizations they comprise.

Going forward, the gap between demographics and regions that have access to modern information and communications technology, and those that do not or have restricted access is only expected to widen. This gap is known as the *digital divide*, and it is important that as professionals we be mindful and conscientious of this gap. There are a variety of reasons why this gap exists: in some areas, access to the right technology and/or the internet is either limited, unavailable, or unaffordable for those who could be equipped. While some may indeed have a reliable internet connection, access to certain digital tools can remain a challenge, just out of reach for those who cannot afford the more expensive tools like laptops and software.

References

Abate, A. F., Guida, M., Leoncini, P., Nappi, M., and Ricciardi, S. (2009). A haptic-based approach to virtual training for aerospace industry. *Journal of Visual Languages & Computing*, 20(5), 318–325.

Adamovich, S. V., Fluet, G. G., Tunik, E., & Merians, A. S. (2009). Sensorimotor training in virtual reality: A review. *NeuroRehabilitation*, 25(1), 29–44.

Aïm, F., Lonjon, G., Hannouche, D., & Nizard, R. (2016). Effectiveness of virtual reality training in orthopaedic surgery. *Arthroscopy: the Journal of Arthroscopic & Related Surgery*, 32(1), 224–232.

Amazon Web Services. (n.d.). What are large language models?https://aws.amazon.com/what-is/large-language-model/.

Baidoo-Anu, D., & Ansah, L. O. (2023). Education in the era of generative artificial intelligence (AI): Understanding the potential benefits of ChatGPT in promoting teaching and learning. *Journal of AI*, 7(1), 52–62.

Bandura, A., & Walters, R. H. (1977). *Social learning theory* (vol. 1). Prentice-Hall.

Bharwaney, R., Martinez, S., Panathula, M., Dalto, J., Maya, A., & Kopasz, L. (2022). Virtual reality in workplace learning: Affordances, limitations, and future directions. *The Journal of Applied Instructional Design*, 11(4).

Center for Creative Leadership. (2020). The 70–20–10 rule for leadership development. www.ccl.org/articles/leading-effectively-articles/70-20-10-rule.

Gavish, N., Gutiérrez, T., Webel, S., Rodríguez, J., Peveri, M., Bockholt, U., & Tecchia, F. (2013). Evaluating virtual reality and augmented reality training for industrial maintenance and assembly tasks. *Interactive Learning Environments*, 23(6), 778–798.

Giurgiu, L. (2017). Microlearning an evolving elearning trend. *Scientific Bulletin*, 22(1), 18–23.

Grantcharov, T. P., Kristiansen, V. B., Bendix, J., Bardram, L., Rosenberg, J., & Funch-Jensen, P. (2004). Randomized clinical trial of virtual reality simulation for laparoscopic skills training. *Journal of British Surgery*, 91(2), 146–150.

Kaplan, A. D., Cruit, J., Endsley, M., Beers, S. M., Sawyer, B. D., & Hancock, P. A. (2021). The effects of virtual reality, augmented reality, and mixed reality as training enhancement methods: A meta-analysis. *Human Factors*, 63(4), 706–726.

Kilteni, K., Groten, R., & Slater, M. (2012). The sense of embodiment in virtual reality. *Presence: Teleoperators and Virtual Environments*, 21(4), 373–387.

Kirschner, P. A. (2017). Stop propagating the learning styles myth. *Computers & Education*, 106, 166–171.

Ma, W., Adesope, O. O., Nesbit, J. C., & Liu, Q. (2014). Intelligent tutoring systems and learning outcomes: A meta-analysis. *Journal of Educational Psychology*, 106(4), 901–918.

Martinez, S. A. & Whiting, J. (2020). Designing informal learning environments. In J. K. McDonald & R. E. West (Eds.), *Design for learning: Principles, processes, and praxis*. EdTech Books.

Nagendran, M., Gurusamy, K. S., Aggarwal, R., Palanivelu, L., & Davidson, B. R. (2013). Virtual reality training for surgical trainees in laparoscopic surgery. *Cochrane Database of Systematic Reviews*, 2013(8), CD006575.

OECD. (2021). Adult learning and COVID-19: How much informal and non-formal learning are workers missing?www.oecd.org/en/publications/adult-learning-and-covid-19-how-much-informal-and-non-formal-learning-are-workers-missing_56a96569-en.html.

Seymour, N. E., Gallagher, A. G., Roman, S. A., O'brien, M. K., Bansal, V. K., Andersen, D. K., & Satava, R. M. (2002). Virtual reality training improves operating room performance: Results of a randomized, double-blinded study. *Annals of Surgery*, 236(4), 458.

Shute, V., & Towle, B. (2003). Adaptive e-learning. *Educational Psychologist*, 38(2), 105–114.

Stanton, J. M., & Barnes-Farrell, J. L. (1996). Effects of electronic performance monitoring on personal control, task satisfaction, and task performance. *Journal of Applied Psychology*, 81(6), 738.

Steinkuehler, C., & Squire, K. (2014). Videogames and learning. In R. K. Sawyer (Ed.), *The Cambridge handbook of the learning sciences* (pp. 377–396). Cambridge University Press.

Stiennon, N., Ouyang, L., Wu, J., Ziegler, D., Lowe, R., Voss, C., Radford, A., Amodei, D., & Christiano, P. (2020). Learning to summarize with human feedback. *Advances in Neural Information Processing Systems*, 33, 3008–3021.

Tlili, A., Shehata, B., Adarkwah, M. A., Bozkurt, A., Hickey, D. T., Huang, R., & Agyemang, B. (2023). What if the devil is my guardian angel: ChatGPT as a case study of using chatbots in education. *Smart Learning Environments*, 10(1), 15.

Vygotsky, L. S. (1978). *Mind in society: The development of higher psychological processes.* Harvard University Press.

Walkington, C. A. (2013). Using adaptive learning technologies to personalize instruction to student interests: The impact of relevant contexts on performance and learning outcomes. *Journal of Educational Psychology*, 105(4), 932.

Wang, S., Christensen, C., Cui, W., Tong, R., Yarnall, L., Shear, L., & Feng, M. (2020). When adaptive learning is effective learning: Comparison of an adaptive learning system to teacher-led instruction. *Interactive Learning Environments*, 31(2), 793–803.

Wang, P., Wu, P., Wang, J., Chi, H. L., & Wang, X. (2018). A critical review of the use of virtual reality in construction engineering education and training. *International Journal of Environmental Research and Public Health*, 15(6), 1204.

Watkins, K. E., & Marsick, V. J. (2021). Informal and incidental learning in the time of COVID-19. *Advances in Developing Human Resources*, 23(1), 88–96.

Watkins, K. E., Marsick, V. J., & de Álava, M. F. (2014). Evaluating informal learning in the workplace. In T. Halttunen, M. Koivisto, & S. Billett (Eds.), *Promoting, assessing, recognizing and certifying lifelong learning: International perspectives and practices* (pp. 59–77). Dordrecht: Springer.

Yan, D., & Fan, Q. (2022). Online informal learning community for interpreter training amid COVID-19: A pilot evaluation. *PLoS One*, 17(11), e0277228.

Zhang, J., & West, R. E. (2020). Designing microlearning instruction for professional development through a competency based approach. *Tech Trends*, 64(2), 310–318.

Index

Page numbers in *italics* and **bold** indicate Figures and Tables, respectively.

Supporting Workplace Learning wi Neuroscience

Supporting Workplace Learning with Neuroscience examines principles of adult learning through the lens of neuroscience and cognitive psychology, effectively demonstrating how this knowledge can be applied in organizational settings to develop professional expertise.

This book opens with three important contextual chapters that unpack the relationship between learning and performance in organizations, the science of developing expertise, and considerations of neurodiversity, culture, and ethics. It goes on to explore the cognitive, behavioral, and socio-emotional dimensions of learning, concluding with tactical chapters that discuss learning through audio-visual channels, key considerations for instructional and learning experience designers, and near-future trends. Each chapter is scaffolded by introductory vignettes and applications for practice, supported by online resources such as PowerPoint instructor slides and suggestions for further reading and resources.

Expertly combining practical insights with theory, this book will be important reading for those studying or researching adult education, while also providing valuable guidance to organizations seeking to support adult learners in the workplace.

Seth-Aaron Martinez is Assistant Professor of Organizational Performance and Workplace Learning at Boise State University, USA. His work centers on expertise development, specifically investigating the expert mental models of individuals (i.e. leaders) and high-performing teams.